READINGS IN NEPALESE ECONOMY

Readings in Nepalese Economy

by

Kamal Raj Dhungel

ADROIT
ADROIT PUBLISHERS
DELHI-110 002

Published by
ADROIT PUBLISHERS
4675/21, Ganpati Bhawan, Ansari Road,
Daryaganj, New Delhi-110 002
Phones : 23266030, 55302465

Distributors
AKHIL BOOK DISTRIBUTORS
e-mail: akhilbooks@yahoo.com
akhilbooks@hotmail.com

ISBN : 81-87392-48-7

Layout
Sudhir Vatsa

Laser Typeset by
Nidhi Laser Point
e-mail: nidhi_vatsa@hotmail.com

Printed in India on behalf of M/s Adroit Publishers by
Arpit Printographers, B-7, Saraswati Complex,
Subhash Chowk, Laxmi Nagar, Delhi-110 092
Phones : 011-33339192, 30971860, 22825424

to my daughter
Nira Dhungel

PREFACE

This book is the outcome of the various articles published in the standard journals and newspapers of Nepal. An attempt of collecting the various contributions made in the study of Nepalese economy from time to time in a single book is thought to provide a great help to the readers. The aim of publishing this book is to provide knowledge to the wide range of readers in both economic theory and its application for practical purposes.

The book comprises of four chapters that provide information of the Nepalese economy and also the factors that affect and have been affecting it.

Considering the immense importance of water resources of Nepal, there are a number of articles related to energy consumption and forecasting. The first chapter of the book is concerned to these issues related to trends and patterns of energy consumption in Nepal. The papers included in this chapter deal with the method of energy demand forecast using econometric models and the same is used to examine the functional relationship between energy consumption and national income taking the time series data of Nepal. The importance of the immense potentiality of water resource and present electricity tariff in the current environment is also examined shortly in two different papers.

Human development and poverty alleviation are the two major challenging concerns of the government of Nepal today. Keeping this in mind, the second chapter of the book outlines the problems inherited in the human development and poverty alleviation and policies and programmes are the key factors of the government to mitigate the inherited problems. Thus in this context, possible programmes, policies and strategies are widely outlined in these papers. In addition in view of designing and framing the macro and micro policies in alleviating poverty is an important aspect. Therefore, attempts are made to provide basic strategies, which may help the government as well as other related institutions in framing policies and programmes to achieve the extreme goal of the poverty alleviation and human resource development.

Economic literature today cannot be separated from the use of mathematics. Mathematical approach to study economic variables has been perceived since the inception of economic theory. Thus, in this respect, chapter three of the book has devoted to the approaches in studying economics by models and mathematical tools. Macro-economic modeling is a necessary step in designing and formulating short-term and long-term periodic plans. Similarly, the design and implementation of the projects, other aspects of the planned development, need to analyze the social cost and benefit. Inequalities measurement and input output analysis are the most important tools in planning. Thus, these mathematical tools are discussed in separate paper giving applications from Nepalese economy.

The last chapter of the book includes the political economy of Nepal. Since 1990, the Nepalese economy is partially being shifted from the state intervention to free market economy. The persisted liberalization of the government is increasing the privatization of state owned industries and corporations at a greater speed. In this light, various papers included in this chapter are related to this theme.

I hope the book will be helpful to the students of Nepali Economy.

January 2004
P.O.Box 19662
Kathmandu, Nepal

Author

Contents

CHAPTER ONE

Energy and Water Resources

1.1 TRENDS AND PATTERNS OF ENERGY CONSUMPTION IN NEPAL: AN ECONOMETRIC APPROACH*

Globally, people have been hearing about energy crisis through the information media since the last three decades. In general, governments of the world have been searching for alternative energy technologies after the OPEC supply shock of Petroleum, Oil and Lubricants (POL) products in 1973. In particular, a great agitation has occurred in the developed countries of the world by the oil embargo because they have been consuming a major share of world oil products. After the oil shock of 1973, both developed and under-developed countries have been giving emphasis on the energy crisis because it is considered that all economic activities are guided by the availability of energy.

Energy is a commodity, which like other commodities, serves to fulfill people's basic needs. Energy is not only needed to fulfill the basic needs of the households where it is used for cooking, heating and lighting but also in transportation, industries, service, agriculture and commercial sectors. Unavailability of adequate energy to fulfill the needs of these sectors will paralyze our economy and it will cease to function properly. Given such a context, it will be

---

* Modified from the original paper published in The Economic Journal of Nepal, Vol. 25, No. 3, 2002, pp. 152-68.

appropriate to quote that:

> "If we were to remove the dollars from our economy, it could continue to function in very different ways. If we were to remove any of the principal commodities say iron ore, fertilizers or trees the economy would continue to function, although again very differently. If energy were removed from the economy, however it would cease to exist once storage were used up."
>
> *(Hall et al. 1986: 21)*

The fact that energy is a commodity has already been stated before. Energy is important not only to consumers, but to producers as well. It acts as a factor of production like land, labour and capital, which is a fact that has been ignored by the neo-classical economists. If we were to remove energy from the production process, labour would be unable to function properly. This can be attributed to the fact that energy is used by the labour in his daily means of subsistence. Land, as a factor of production, will not be fertile (to grow trees, crops, etc.) without energy. Land absorbs heat from the sun, which is sufficient to become fertile. Capital, another important factor of production, cannot be manufactured without availability of energy. Therefore, so important is energy and its intensity so great that it determines the efficiency of the labour and capital involved in the production process.

The main focus of this article is on the consumption of commercial energy. An attempt is made to fit an exponential trend, taking time as independent variable and energy consumption in GJ as the dependent variable. However, this attempt is limited to the consumption of commercial energy. It is because of the availability of the data concerning the consumption of biomass fuel being either inadequate or inappropriate. The method of least squares will be used to estimate the energy consumption from historical data. The semi-log linear regression equation would be:

1. $\ln TDEC = \alpha_0 + \alpha_1 t$
2. $\ln CEC = \alpha_0 + \alpha_1 t$
3. $\ln CC = \alpha_0 + \alpha_1 t$

4. $\ln PPC = \alpha_0 + \alpha_1 t$
5. $\ln EC = \alpha_0 + \alpha_1 t$

where,

TDEC = Traditional Energy Consumption (fuelwood, agricultural waste, animal dung)
CEC = Commercial Energy Consumption
CC = Coal Consumption
PPC = Petroleum Products Consumption
EC = Electricity Consumption.
T = time period at origin 1984/85 = 1

ENERGY SITUATION OF NEPAL

Water and Energy Commission (WECS) 1996 has estimated that Nepal's per capita final energy consumption 6 is 15GJ (Giga Joules). It reflects that the energy consumption per capita is low. The level of economic development is largely determined by per capita energy consumption and hence this indicator shows the living standard of people. The World Bank (2000/01) estimates that Nepal's per capita GNP is equivalent to US dollar 220 and that 51 per cent of the total population lives under absolute poverty with an income less than one dollar a day (World Bank: 2000/01; UNDP 2000). This is the scenario now Nepal is facing. The main source of energy in Nepal is biomass that accounts for over 90 per cent of the total energy consumption. The historical trend of energy consumption by fuel type is presented in Annex.

To relate our society to energy use it is necessary to analyze different strata of the people in the society. Over 86 per cent of the population lives in the rural areas and their livelihood is based on agriculture. Recently, it is partly diverted to other sectors; also there is high labour mobility outside the country. The rural people earn some money as a remittance derived from other countries of the world. There is a wide variation between the distribution of income, consumption patterns, attitudes, aspirations and life styles of the people in Nepal. The above variables separate the elites of Nepal from the masses. There is a great disparity in the energy consumption pattern of the people as there is a disparity in the income, consumption, attitudes, aspirations and life style of Nepali people.

Fuelwood has always been the dominant source of energy in Nepal. It fulfils over 80 per cent of the primary energy requirements of the people. The major sources of fuelwood are public forests, shrub lands, grasslands and private holdings. The annual growth rate of fuelwood consumption during 1984/85—1994/95 was 2 per cent. Fuelwood is likely to remain the principal source of energy in the foreseeable future. However, it is important to note that the depletion of forests is the major concern of the recent times. The growing demand of firewood coupled with the mismanagement of its sources is exhausting the forest cover and resulting in

(*a*) increased usage of agricultural waste and the same of animal dung. (These increased with a growth rate of 4.5 per cent and 1.3 per cent per annum during 1984/85–1994/95 respectively). Increased usage of animal dung as primary source of energy directly imposes adverse effect in agricultural productivity because it is used as a source of energy rather than a supplement to crop as fertilizer.

(*b*) environmental degradation through soil erosion, and

(*c*) increased wastage of manpower in gathering firewood.

Forest resources, a major source of energy, has dwindled over time due to continuous extraction for domestic and commercial use. WECS (1994/95) has estimated a total forest and shrub land of 4520.94 thousand hectares of which 2127.81 thousand hectares are accessed for fuel wood collection. While making this estimation, it has been assumed that the rate of depletion is 2 per cent per annum.

As for the availability of commercial energy source Nepal has no proven deposits of fossil fuel. The use of fossil fuel as energy is growing substantially at present and it is expected that it will grow at a faster rate in the near future. The imported hydrocarbons are used as energy not only for transportation, industrial and other requirements but also for domestic cooking and lighting. Hydrocarbon imports contribute to a significant proportion of the country's import bill. The total amount of hydrocarbon imports is about 226 thousand tonnes per annum *(Ramani, et al.: 1993).*

While dealing with the situation of energy consumption in Nepal, it is necessary to analyze various factors, which are economic in nature. Energy consumption is affected by many factors, the main ones are population size, GDP per capita, prices charged for energy (particularly for POL products), the structure of the economy including the energy intensity of different sectors and particularly the average temperature of winter season *(Gamba, et al.1986).* However, this chapter does not attempt to take all these factors under consideration. Energy consumption in Nepal is presented in the following table on the basis of energy sources.

TABLE 1.1
Annual growth rate of Energy Consumption in different periods

(in percent)

Energy sources	*1984/85-1989/90*	*1989/90-1995/96*	*1995/96-2000/01*
Fuelwood	1.2	2.2	2.7
Agriculture waste	2.8	2.2	2.7
Animal dung	2.6	2.2	2.5
Coal	-14.2	6.9	27.2
Petroleum	7.8	12.6	12.7
Electricity	17.5	8.7	10.4
Total	2.7	2.8	3.9

Source: Economic survey, MOF/HMG, 2001.

The overall annual growth rate of energy consumption during 1984/85–1989/90 was 2.7 per cent (Table 1). The annual growth rate of fuelwood, agriculture waste, animal dung, coal, petroleum and electricity were 1.2, 2.8, 2.6, -14.2, 7.8 and 17.5 respectively. The annual growth rate of coal remained negative meaning that the coal consumption as energy during this period of time had decreased. However, the annual growth rate of coal consumption increased and reached 6.9 and 27.2 per cent during 1989/90–1995/96 and 1995/96–2000/01 respectively. The annual growth rate of petroleum product was 7.8 per cent during (1984/85–1989/90). However, it increased alarmingly during the periods of 1989/90-1995/96 and 1995/96–2000/01. During these periods the annual growth rate remained 12.6 and 12.7 per cent respectively. The annual growth rate of electricity was 17.5 per cent during the period of 1984/85–1989/90. During 1989/90–1995/96 the growth rate of electricity dwindled to 8.7 per cent. However, the annual growth rate of electricity increased and reached 10.4 per cent during the period 1995/96–2001/01.

TABLE 1.2
Energy Consumption

(in thousand Tons of Oil Equivalent; TOE)

Energy sources	*1984/85*	*%*	*1989/90*	*%*	*1995/96*	*%*	*2000/01*	*%*
Fuelwood	4269	84.8	4753	84.8	5408	81.9	6165	77.2
Ag. Waste	191	3.8	213	3.8	243	3.7	278	3.5
Anm. Dung	320	6.4	355	6.3	404	6.1	457	5.7
Coal	83	1.6	45	0.8	67	1.0	223	2.7
POL	151	3.0	204	3.6	416	6.3	756	9.5
Electricity	21	0.4	40	0.7	66	1.0	108	1.4
Total	5035	100	5610	100	6604	100	7987	100

Source: Economic Survey, MOF/HMG, 2001.

Energy consumption in Nepal is dominated by traditional sources. Traditional sources of energy accounted for 95, 94.9, 91.7 and 86.4 per cent of which fuelwood alone contributed to 84.5, 84.8, 81.9 and 77.2 per cent in 1984/85, 1989/90, and 1995/96 and 2000/01 respectively. The share of commercial energy consumption was 5, 5.1, 8.3 and 13.6 during these periods. The per capita commercial energy consumption is very low revealing the low level of economic development.

Analysis of Energy Consumption Over Time

The trend line equation has been estimated using time series data (Annex 3). The regression equations are estimated for each type of energy used. For traditional sources total energy consumption is considered whereas for commercial sources various sources are treated separately. The following table shows the results of the regression equations:

TABLE 1.3
Fuelwise Estimation of Regression Equation

Equation	α_0	*t-stat*	α_1	*t-stat*	*F*	R^2
1	12.2	2331.3	0.02	31.98	1022.9	0.99
2	9.0	103.2	0.094	7.36	54.21	0.85
3	7.08	13.39	0.06	0.79	0.63	0.06
4	8.6	158.41	0.11	13.54	183.33	0.95
5	6.91	180.7	0.09	17.64	311.4	0.97

Biomass Fuel

It includes the consumption of fuelwood, agricultural waste and animal dung. The annual growth rate of biomass consumption in Nepal during 1984/85–1994/95 was 2 per cent. The result of the first regression equation is obtained by taking time as an independent variable and consumption of biomass in Nepal as the dependent variable. From the result, the growth rate is inelastic, meaning any change in the time will have less than unitary (proportionate) change on the consumption of biomass. It is because there is no fuel substitution (for cooking, heating etc.). The value of R^2 is very high meaning that 99 per cent change in the biomass consumption is explained by the equation. The overall fit of the exponential trend of the historical energy consumption data over time is highly significant for the reason that the F-ratio, as we have seen in the table, is very high.

Commercial Energy Consumption

Coming to the consumption of commercial energy, Nepal has no proven source of hydrocarbons. Electricity is only the indigenous source of commercial energy in Nepal. This high growth rate of commercial energy consumption in Nepal can be attributed to the increased number of vehicles, urbanization and promotion of industrial activities. The growth rate is inelastic meaning any change in time will have less than unitary (proportionate) change in the consumption of commercial energy. It is because there is no fuel substitution for transport. R^2 is 0.85 meaning that the model explains 85 per cent change in the commercial energy consumption in Nepal.

Coal

The third regression equation is related to the consumption of coal in Nepal. There was a declining trend of coal consumption during 1984/85–1994/95 (–2.2 percent). For this reason the value of r^2 is insignificant. However, the regression coefficients are positive indicating that there is a positive relationship between coal consumption and time. The overall significance of the fit of the regression equation seems very thin.

Petroleum Products

The overriding increase in the use of petroleum products has been conceived from the viewpoint of increased number of vehicles, rapid urbanization, expansion of road facilities and the changes in the lifestyle of the people. The annual growth rate of consumption of petroleum products during 1984/85–1994/95 was 9.5 per cent. If this growth rate of petroleum products continues in the future, Nepal has to pay substantial amount of foreign currency it earns to meet the demand of POL products. The fourth regression equation has been established to show the trend of consumption of petroleum products over time. R^2 is highly significant that 95 per cent change in petroleum product consumption has been explained by the change in time. The coefficient is 0.11 meaning that the changes in time say, by one year; the petroleum products will be changed by 11 per cent. F-ratio is high enough to justify overall significance of the estimated regression equation. It shows that in Nepal, the petroleum products import will increase substantially causing an unfavourable trade balance as well as a similar balance of payments.

Electricity

The only indigenous commercial source of energy in Nepal, electricity, at present contributes less than one per cent of the total energy consumption. The hydropower potential in Nepal is about 83 thousand MW of which 25 thousand MW is economically feasible. However, the production of hydropower is less than one per cent of the total hydropower potential. The annual growth rate of electricity consumption during 1984/85–1994/95 was 9.1 per cent. At present, about 14 per cent of the population has access to electricity (Ninth plan).

The fifth regression equation establishes a relationship between electricity consumption and time. The estimated slope coefficient is found to be 0.09. Changes in time are positively related to electricity consumption. The annual growth rate of electricity demand is about 9 per cent. This highlights the importance of electricity consumption over the change in time. R^2 is high enough to justify that 97 per cent change in electricity consumption has been associated with the time. The overall significance of the estimated trend is appreciable for the reason that F-ratio is seemed very high.

Energy and National Output

Economic production has been defined as the process in which fuel, capital and labour are combined to transform natural resources into goods and services produced. The quality of these products ultimately depends on the quantity of economic energy available and the efficiency with which that energy is used *(Hall et al. 1986)*. However, the principal concern of this article is not to establish such relationship between energy use and GDP. But it is certainly true that the principal concern here is to relate energy use to total economic output that may effect income elasticity. In this context, focus will be given to calculate income elasticity with the help of the following models:

(a) $\text{In TCEC} = \alpha_0 + \alpha_1 \text{ In GDP}$

(b) $\text{In PPC} = \alpha_0 + \alpha_1 \text{ In GDP}$

(c) $\text{In EC} = \alpha_0 + \alpha_1 \text{ In GDP}$

where,

TCEC = Total Commercial Energy Consumption in thousand TOE.

PPC = Petroleum Product Consumption in thousand TOE.

EC = Electricity Consumption in thousand TOE.

GDP = Gross Domestic Product at real prices (1984/85 = 100)

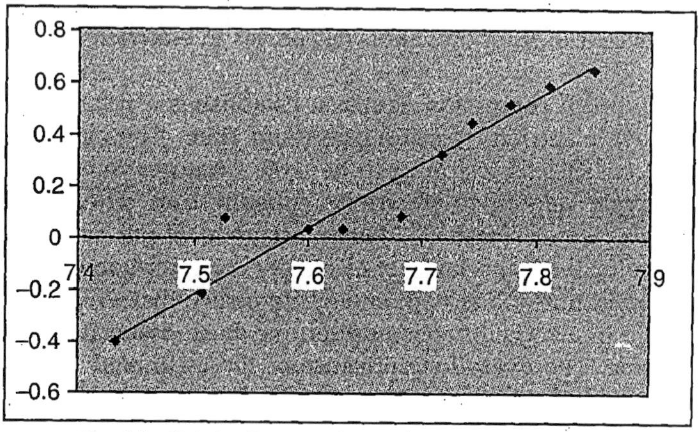

Fig. 1.1 : Relation Between Commercial Energy and GDP

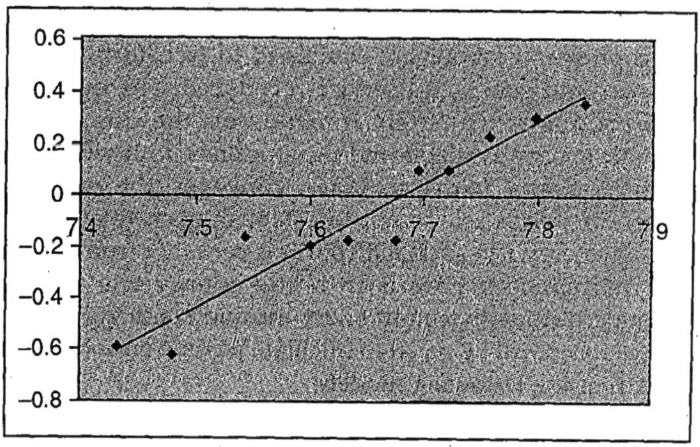

Fig. 1.2 : The relationship between POL products and GDP

The estimation technique of the above regression equations is the method of least square. The values of the variables are expressed in per capita terms. Following diagrams show the relationship between energy used and GDP in Nepal during 1991-2001.

The GDP in real prices and energy consumption is measured in x and y axis respectively in the diagrams 1.1,1.2 and1.3.

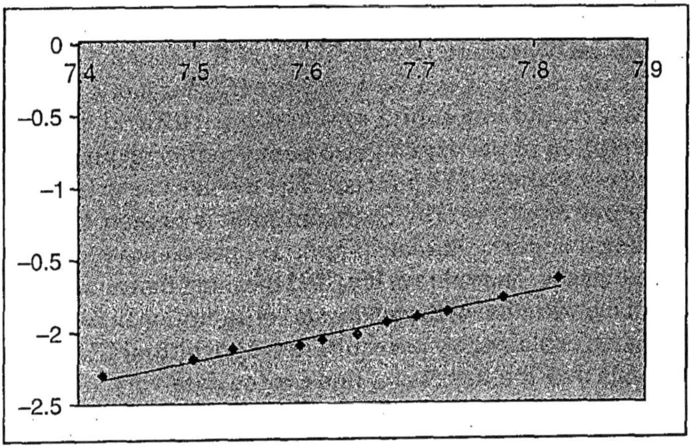

Fig. 1.3: Relationship between Electricity Consumption and GDP

The regression coefficients of the above models are presented in the table below:

TABLE 1.4

Income elasticity of per capita energy consumption

Energy sources	*Estimated slope coefficients*	R^2	*T-values*
Total Commercial Energy	2.69	0.95	13.13
Petroleum Product	1.74	0.92	10.44
Electricity	1.49	0.95	14.63

First of all let us deal with the income elasticity of total commercial energy consumption in Nepal. From these regression results (table 4) we know that the income elasticity coefficient is 2.69. It implies that for a one per cent increase in the per capita real non-agricultural GDP the total per capita commercial energy consumption on an average increases by about 2.69 per cent. Since the income elasticity of per capita energy consumption is greater than one, we can say that per capita commercial energy consumption is income elastic. The value of R^2 shows the fit of the regression line implying that about 95 per cent of the variation of the per capita commercial energy consumption is explained by per capita non-agricultural GDP.

Similarly, the income elasticity of the consumption of petroleum products is 1.74. It implies that for a one per cent increase in the per capita real non-agricultural GDP the consumption of per capita petroleum product on an average increases by about 1.74 per cent. The income elasticity of per capita petroleum product consumption is greater than one meaning that per capita consumption of petroleum products is income elastic. The value of R^2 is 0.92 meaning that about 92 per cent of the variation of the per capita consumption of petroleum product is explained by per capita non-agricultural GDP. It also suggests that the regression line fits the data very well.

Coming to per capita electricity consumption, the estimated coefficient is low as compared to the per capita consumption of petroleum products. It is an amazing fact that despite Nepal's high potential of hydropower generation, electricity could not contribute a significant amount to total energy consumption. However, the income elasticity of the consumption of electricity is positive as well as greater than one. The value of the income elasticity of the per capita electricity consumption is 1.49. It implies that for a one per cent increase in the per capita real non-agricultural GDP the per capita electricity consumption, on an average increases by about 1.49 per cent. The value of R^2 is 0.95 suggesting that the regression line fits the data very well. It implies that, about 95 per cent of the variation of per capita electricity consumption is explained by per capita non-agricultural GDP. The income elasticity of the per capita consumption of electricity is income elastic.

Forecast of Energy Consumption

The estimated relationship between energy consumption and time can be used to forecast energy consumption. Of course, one needs to estimate future levels of real GDP and population prior to use the estimated equations to forecast energy consumption. However, assuming the present constant growth rate of real GDP as well as population makes the energy forecasting for future. It is assumed that the annual growth rate of population will remain 2.24 per cent per annum and the real GDP growth rate will be around 4 per cent per annum. Given this constant growth rate of population and real GDP, the future energy is estimated with the base of the energy consumption data of 1994/95.

TABLE 1.5
Estimated Energy Consumption

(in million Gj)

Energy Type	*1994/95*	*2004/05*	*2014/15*	*Growth Rate (1994/95–2014/15)*
Biomass	262.3	302.5	369.5	1.7
Commercial	23.1	58.3	149.3	9.8
Coal	2.8	4.2	7.6	5.1
POL products	17.5	54.7	164.4	11.9
Electricity	2.8	6.6	16.3	9.1
Total	308.5	426.3	707.1	4.2

The energy estimated results already show an increasing trend of consumption of energy in Nepal. Biomass fuel energy will increase at an annual growth rate of 1.7 per cent during 1994/95-2014/15. The consumption of biomass fuel was 262.3 million GJ in 1994/95 and estimated value shows it will reach 369.5 million GJ in 2014/15. There will remain a high annual growth rate of the consumption of commercial energy during the same period of time. It increases at 9.8 per cent per annum. The consumption of commercial energy was 23.1 million GJ in1994/95. It will reach 149.3 million GJ in 2014/15. There is six-fold increase in the consumption of commercial energy during 1984/85 to 2014/15. The past trend shows that there is a declining trend in the consumption of coal. However, in the coming years the coal consumption in Nepal will increase by an annual growth rate of 5.1 per cent. It is observed that there is a higher annual growth rate of the consumption of imported hydrocarbons in Nepal. It is expected that the continuation of imported hydrocarbons at this rate of growth per annum, Nepal will face acute problem in its balance of payments that will occur from the high degree of trade deficit. There is only one option to keep the consumption of imported hydrocarbons intact. Nepal should generate substantial quantity of hydro-electricity from its abundant water resources and sell to other countries that can generate foreign currency in order to solve the acute balance of payment problem. If this step is not taken seriously under consideration, Nepal should reduce the consumption of imported hydrocarbons to minimum level. There will be nine-fold increase in the consumption of hydrocarbons during 1994/95–2014/15. Similarly, the historical fact shows that there is an increasing trend in the consumption of electricity in Nepal that need to generate additional elasticity by investing huge amount of money in this sector.

From table 5, it is observed that the total energy consumption will increase at an annual growth rate of 4.2 per cent. The consumption of energy in 2014/15 will be more than double to that of the consumption of energy in 1994/95.

Conclusion

There has been growing concern recently about energy consumption, energy security and energy conservation. Oil shock of 1970's hit the world today and many of the developed and under-developed countries have been trying to innovate alternative permanent source of energy. Nepal is no exception of the event although it consumes an insignificant quantity of petroleum products. However, Nepal is paying one-third merchandise export earnings to import hydrocarbons per annum. High population growth rate of Nepal demands more farmland for which forest land of

Nepal is being converted into agricultural land. In addition, people depend on firewood to meet their primary energy requirement for which the forests in Nepal are dwindling overtime. Past trend shows that the growth of GDP is closely related to growth rate of energy consumption in Nepal. The energy-GDP elasticity is found highly elastic. Taking historical growth rate of GDP and population, the energy demand forecast has been made. Nepal has low level of per capita commercial energy consumption. Imported hydrocarbons contributes a major share in the commercial energy consumption in Nepal. Electric energy does not have significant impact in the total commercial energy consumption although electric energy elasticity is found to be significant. The high economic growth rate can be achieved when the economy is endowed with adequate energy. The growth rate of economy, among other things primarily depends on the availability of energy in an economy. Nepal is rich in water resources and hydro-electricity is the only indigenous source of commercial energy. Its development and generation has remained stagnant since last because of the long debating proposals of Arun III to Mahakali Package Program. While dealing with the energy consumption in Nepal, the second set of regression equation shows that there is a strong relationship between energy consumption and economic development. The elasticity coefficients are greater than one. This fact reveals that an increase in per capita real GDP will increase the amount of per capita energy consumption. The future energy consumption is made with the help of first set of regression equations, which reveals that energy consumption in Nepal will increase over time.

1.2 ENERGY DEMAND FORECASTS: ISSUES AND OPTIONS*

Literally, as well as practically, to forecast is to predict future events or actions. The predictor generally takes past values

* *Modified from the original paper published in* The Economic Journal of Nepal, Vol. 24, No. 4, 2001, pp. 196-211.

as the basis of forecasting. Forecasts of the future events are based on certain assumptions. For all forecasts involve some kind of uncertainty. Using regression analysis generally makes predictions of future events on the basis of past values. It requires variables of two types: dependent variable that are to be forecasted and independent or explanatory variable which is the basis of forecasting.

To forecast the former on the basis of the latter variables, the predictor either uses time series data or cross-sectional data. Regression analysis expresses the casual relationship between two or more than two variables under consideration.

Time series data reflects the values in a chronological sequence of observations of a particular variable. In time series models, historical data on the variable to be forecasted is analyzed in an attempt to identify a data pattern. The forecaster then may assume that this pattern will continue in the future. Extrapolation of data is necessary in order to forecast. While modeling time series data, the basic assumption is that the data pattern that has been identified will persist in the future. In casual models, the assumption is that the relationship between the dependent variable will hold. Uncertainty arises in casual model forecasting because assumption must be made on the values of the independent variable before a forecast can be made.

Following are the basic sectors, which have to be considered in choosing a forecasting technique:

(a) The objective of forecasting
(b) The time frame
(c) The pattern of data
(d) The cost of forecasting .
(e) The accuracy desired
(f) The ease of operation and understanding.

Trend Analysis

Time series data involves an increasing or decreasing pattern of values over time. The smoothly increasing or decreasing pattern of data is said to contain a trend. Various time series data such as energy consumption, GDP, GNP and other related indicators appear to be in a trend. These trends appear due to increase in population, improvements in technology and increase in wealth or combinations of these effects. One can make use of this trending behaviour of data. Trend analysis uses mathematical formulae to fit a past series of values with time. Projections are then made by extrapolation. The data may be first transformed before it is used for curve fitting. Thus, in this light, trend analysis is a time series forecasting method.

The trending behaviour of the time series data requires some mathematical formulae to fit a past series of values with time as independent variable. There are some uncertainties to use trend analysis in forecasting:

1. It makes no attempt to discover the factors affecting the behaviour of the system.
2. It may be extremely difficult to measure the relationship.
3. The major concern may be only to predict what will happen and not to know why it happens.

Estimating a Curve

Various growth curves can be used to fit the trending data. However, in common practice simple curves such as a straight-line on an exponential are used to fit the data. For data tending to saturation level, growth curves are normally used. Some of the commonly used trends are shown in the figure 1.4 on page 18.

From the Fig. 1.4 is seen that in several cases a unique curve is not a possibility. In such a situation, the user can fit all the possible curves under consideration. After fitting the possible curves, the user can examine which curve gives the best fit. The most commonly used curve fitting technique is the ordinary least square (OLS) method. However, various non-linear curve fitting technique are also available. For these non-linear curve-fitting techniques, it is possible to make them linear by logarithmic transformation. The user can follow this procedure to apply the OLS method.

There are numerous mathematical formulae to be used

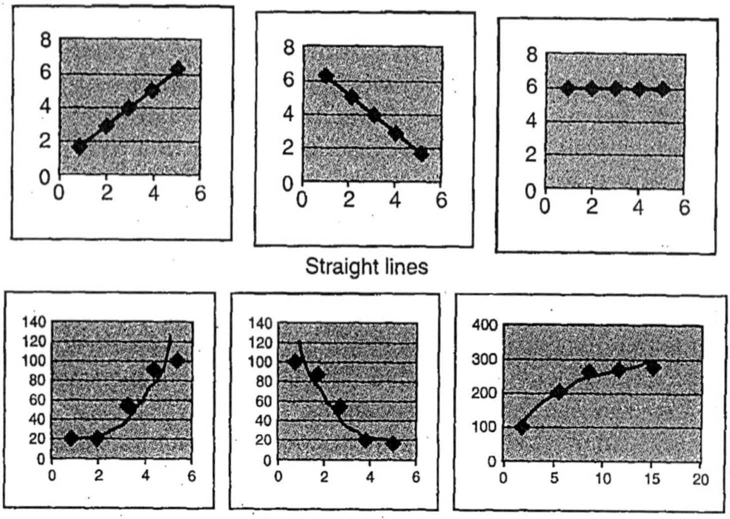

Exponential Curves

FIG. 1.4 : Possible shapes of the curves with time trend.

to analyze trending. Some of them are chosen here to represent the theoretical trends. The following formulae contains few parameters, which may be the good candidates:

(a)	The straight line:	y=a+bt
(b)	The exponential curve:	y=exp(a+bt)
(c)	The parabolic curve:	y=a+bt+ct^2
(d)	The modified exponential curve:	y=s+a exp (bt)
(e)	The Gompertz curve:	y=s*exp[a*exp(bt)]
(f)	The logistic curve:	y=s/[1+a*exp(bt)]

where,

y — is the time series of interest.
t — is the time.
s — is the saturation level, and
a,b,c are formulae parameters.

The above formulae can be transformed in the semi-logarithmic form in order to apply the OLS method because this process gives linearity to the dependent variable. Some of the examples of semi-log transformation are shown below:

(i) In y = a + bt
(ii) In (y-s) = In a + bt

(*iii*) In [In (s/y)] = In a + bt
(*iv*) In (s/y-1) = In a + bt

In the last three equations it is assumed that saturation level is known. If the value of *s* is not known and it is treated as a parameter to be estimated, non-linear fitting need to be used.

The Application of Trend Analysis in Energy Demand

Here, an attempt is made to show the example of trend analysis in the energy demand analysis. In Nepal the consumption of electricity has increased exponentially over the last decade. The exponential growth trend can easily be detected if the consumption is plotted against time. There is a strong correlation between per capita energy consumption and per capita non-agricultural GDP. The time series data of per capita electricity consumption and per capita non-agricultural GDP between 1991and 2001 of Nepalese economy is plotted in logarithmic scale which is shown in Fig. 1.5.

The 1991–2001 data is used to fit the following selected simple models:

$$Ln(EC) = a+bt \qquad ...(1)$$

$$Ln(EC) = a+bln(NGDP) \qquad ...(2)$$

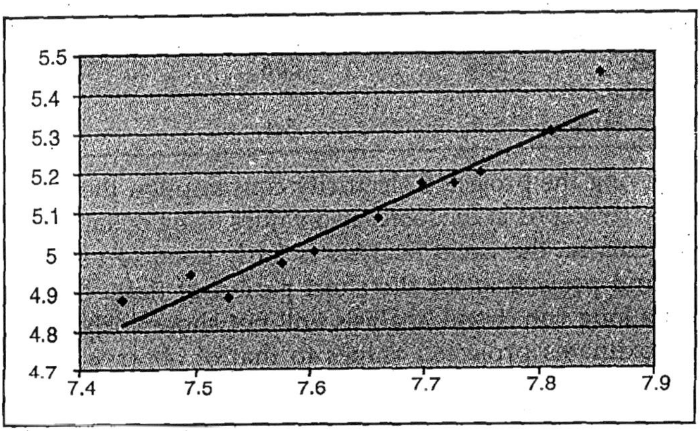

Fig.1.5: Per capita Electricity Consumption and per capita non-agricultural GDP

$$Ln(NGDP) = a+bt \quad ...(3)$$

where,

EC = Electricity Consumption (in million GJ)

T = Time

NGDP = Non-agricultural GDP (in million Rupees)

The estimated equations are given below:

$$Ln(EC) = 4.77 + 0.059t \quad ...(4) \quad r^2 = 0.92$$

$$Ln(NGDP) = 7.43 + 0.038t \quad ...(5) \quad r^2 = 0.99$$

$$Ln(EC) = -5.5 + 1.4\ ln(NGDP) \quad ...(6) \quad r^2 = 0.90$$

Based on the r^2 values the models give fairly good fits. The estimated electricity consumption and non-agricultural GDP are given in the following table:

TABLE 1.6
Projected Electricity Consumption

(in GJ and NGDP)

Year	*Using Equation 4*	*Using Equation 5*	*Using Equation 6*
2002	239	240	2643
2003	254	253	2744
2004	269	267	2849
2005	286	281	2958
2006	303	296	3071
2007	322	312	3189
2008	341	329	3311
2009	362	347	3438
2010	384	366	3570
Av. Annual growth rates	5.5	5.4	3.8

Observing the projected electricity consumption there are no much variations in the forecasted values using equation 4 and 5. Therefore, the trend analysis is fairly good to use energy demand projection for the short period of time. However, in the long run, trend analysis will not show fairly good or approximates projected values to that of observed values. The second and third columns show projected per capita electricity consumption and last column represents the projected per capita non-agricultural GDP.

Energy Consumption and Economic Growth

Nepal's energy consumption is characterized by a low level of per capita consumption. WECS estimated it at about 14 GJ. In terms of commercial energy consumption, Nepal has high growth rate. The table 1.7 (Fig. 1.6), shows that during the period 1990-93, approximately 27 per cent increase in commercial energy consumption has been observed. When comparing with the growth rates of energy consumption and economic growth; the growth rate of total energy consumption is less than the GDP growth rate.

When the growth rate of energy consumption is viewed to that of the growth rate of GDP in Nepal during (1985–2001) the growth rate of CSC has the greater growth rate then the GDP growth. During the period 1986-89, the growth rate of commercial energy consumption is slightly lesser than the growth of GDP. However, it is a surprising fact that during the period 1990-93, Commercial energy consumption increased at 5.6 times the growth rate of GDP and followed 1.5 times and 2.5 times the growth of GDP during the period 1994-97, and 1998-2001 respectively.

TABLE 1.7
The Growth rate of Energy Consumption and GDP

Particulars	*1986-89*	*1990-93*	*1994-97*	*1998-2001*
Real GDP	4.8	4.8	5.3	5.0
Total Energy consumption	2.2	3.0	2.7	3.9
Commercial energy consumption	4.3	26.9	8.6	12.6

Relationship Between Electricity Consumption and Non-agricultural GDP

A standard of measuring economic activity is essential for examining the relation between national fuel use and the production of material goods. To examine between energy (electricity) consumption and national output here, an attempt is made to show the relationship between energy (electricity) consumption and non-agricultural GDP as the output. The performance of an economy is primarily based on the availability of commercial energy. Electricity is only the indigenous source of Nepal. Nepal is the second richest country after Brazil with respect to water resources. Owning such vast hydropower potential (83000MW), less than one per cent of it is utilized. Accessibility of electricity is limited to 14 per cent of the population of Nepal. However, the accessibility of electricity is again limited to the urban population of the country. Electricity contributes 1.4 per cent and 9.9 per cent to total energy consumption and total commercial energy consumption in the fiscal year 2000/01 respectively.

The Energy Efficiency

Energy efficiency is a concept used differently by different users. It has a variety of meanings depending on the perspectives of the observer. Economists define efficiency in relation to pereto optimality, which is the pattern of allocation of scarce resources so that no one can be made better off without making someone else worse off.

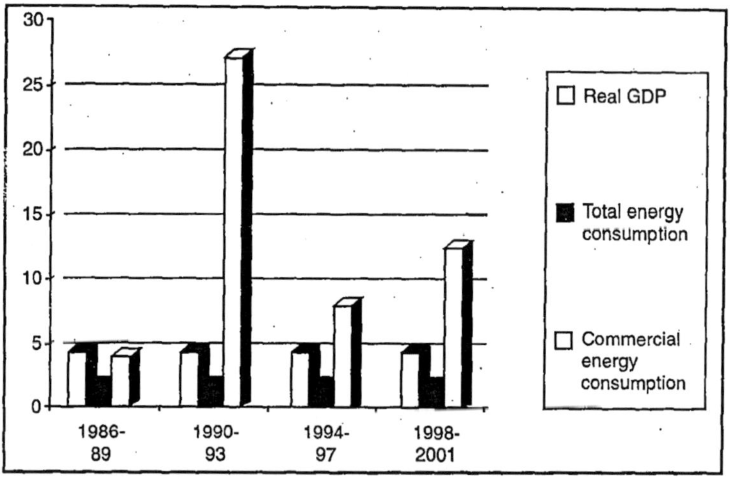

Source: Economic Survey, 2001.

Fig. 1.6: The growth rate of Energy Consumption and GDP

Accordingly, efficiency is defined in terms of the quantity of fuel used to provide a unit of economic output. Thus, the most commonly used index of an economic system's energy efficiency is the ratio of fuel used by that system in a given period to the real GNP produced during that period.

$$\text{Thus, Energy efficiency} = \frac{\text{Total fuel used in period } t}{\text{GDP produced in period } t}$$

To keep this concept into practice, an attempt is made to calculate electricity consumption efficiency in Neplaese economy. The electricity consumption and non-agricultural GDP during 1984/85–2000/01 has been taken to calculate the energy (electricity) efficiency.

The time series data is used to find the energy (electricity) efficiency. The data is taken from the secondary sources.

TABLE 1.8
Energy (electricity) Efficiency in Nepalese Economy

Year	*Efficiency*	*Year*	*Efficiency*	*Year*	*Efficiency*
1985	0.014	1991	0.021	1997	0.022
1986	0.015	1992	0.021	1998	0.021
1987	0.017	1993	0.021	1999	0.022
1988	0.018	1994	0.020	2000	0.023
1989	0.018	1995	0.020	2001	0.026
1990	0.019	1996	0.021		

Electricity Intensity of KWh per 1 million rupees.

The average energy (electricity) intensity in Nepalese economy has been only two per cent per annum during 1985-2001. This low energy (electricity) intensity has been attributed to the following reasons:

1. The tariff of electricity in Nepal is very low compared to the cost of electricity production. Due to the low level of price per unit the producers as well as consumers do not care about its consumption efficiently. The producers use obsolete machineries in their factories that consume huge units of

electricity when they are in the operation. Similarly, the consumers are also using electricity inefficiently due to low tariff, which does not give burden feelings to them.

2. There is the loss of one-fourth of total electric power every year in Nepal. Loss of power is mainly due to the inefficiency in the transmission and distribution of line.

Energy-Income Elasticity

Now, I am turning to estimate the energy income elasticity in Nepalese economy. Despite the lack of adequate data, attempt is made to fit the following type of models taking time series data of the period 1985-99:

$$\text{Ln TEC} = \alpha_0 + \alpha_1 \text{lnr GDP} \quad \text{....1}$$

$$\text{Ln TEC} = \alpha_0 + \alpha_1 \text{lnr GDP} + \alpha_2 \text{lnN} \quad \text{....2}$$

$$\text{Ln CEC} = \alpha_0 + \alpha_1 \text{lnr NGDP} \quad \text{....3}$$

$$\text{Ln CEC} = \alpha_0 + \alpha_1 \text{lnr NGDP} + \alpha_2 \text{lnN} \quad \text{....4}$$

$$\text{Ln EC} = \alpha_0 + \alpha_1 \text{lnr NGDP} \quad \text{....5}$$

$$\text{In EC} = \alpha_0 + \alpha_1 \text{lnr NGDP} + \alpha_2 \text{lnN} \quad \text{....6}$$

where,

TEC = Per capita total energy consumption (in GJ)

CEC = Per capita commercial energy consumption (in GJ)

EC = per capita commercial energy consumption (in KW)

RGDP = Per capita real GDP

RNGDP = Per capita non-agricultural real GDP

N = Population

α_0, α_1 and α_2 are the parameters, and

α_1 signifies the energy income elasticity.

Empirical Results

The estimated values of each of the models is presented in the following table:

TABLE 1.9

Estimated results of the equations 1, 2, 3, 4, 5 and 6

Model	α_0	*t-stat*	α_1	*t-stat*	*F*	R^2
1	2.41	37.08	0.023	3.08	9.98	0.42
2	1.45	5.42	–0.11	–2.99	15.75	0.72
3	–13.7	–9.2	1.82	9.13	83.4	0.87
4	–11.8	–2.96	0.90	0.57	39.5	0.87
5	–11.23	–5.58	1.21	4.49	20.12	0.61
6	–14.5	–2.12	1.35	0.56	9.92	0.61

In model (1), total energy consumption (including traditional and commercial) is considered. From the model it is found that the income elasticity coefficient is 0.0023. It implies that for a one per cent increase in the per capita GDP the total per capita energy consumption on an average increases by about 0.0023 per cent. Since the income elasticity of per capita income elasticity is less than one, we can say that per capita total energy consumption is income inelastic. The value of r^2 shows the fit of the model implying that only about 42 per cent of the variation of the per capita total energy consumption is explained by per capita real GDP.

Model 1 shows inelastic value of income elasticity.

Model 2 incorporates population as an explanatory variable. It captures the effect on income elasticity via a population. However there is no improvement in income elasticity. R^2 is 0.72, which shows the fit of the model. However, the elasticity coefficient is negative. It reveals that there is no improvement in income elasticity.

Model 3 incorporates the per capita commercial energy consumption as dependent variable and per capita real GDP as an explanatory variable. From the above table it is found that elasticity coefficient is 1.83. It implies that for a one per cent increase in the per capita real non-agricultural GDP total per capita energy consumption on an average increases by about 1.83 per cent. Since the income elasticity of per capita energy consumption is greater than one, we can say that per capita commercial energy consumption is income elastic. The value of the r^2 shows the fit of the model implying that about

87 per cent of the variation of the per capita commercial energy consumption is explained by per capita non-agricultural GDP.

Using model 4 to the same with population as an additional explanatory variable, it is found that the coefficient of income elasticity is less than one. There is no improvement in the value of income elasticity. However, the value of coefficient of determination remains the same.

Model 5 incorporates the per capita electricity consumption as a dependent variable and per capita real non-agricultural GDP as an explanatory variable. From the table it is seen that the estimated coefficient is low as compared to the per capita consumption of total commercial energy consumption. It is an amazing fact that despite Nepal's high potential of hydropower generation, electricity could not contribute a significant amount to total commercial energy consumption.

However, the income elasticity of the consumption of electricity is positive as well as greater than one. The coefficient of income elasticity of the per capita electricity consumption is 1.21. It implies that for a one per cent increase in the per capita real non-agricultural GDP, the per capita electricity consumption on an average increases by about 1.21 per cent. In this model, it is found that the value of coefficient of determination is moderate. It is found only 0.61 and suggesting that 61 per cent of the variation of per capita electricity consumption is explained by per capita non-agricultural GDP. However, the coefficient shows that the income elasticity of the per capita electricity consumption is income elastic.

Now turning to last model, there is an additional explanatory variable (i.e population). Three variables under consideration are correlated. There is an improvement in the value of income elasticity compared to the value of model 5. In this model, the coefficient of income elasticity is 1.35 while the value of coefficient of income elasticity is 1.21, while the value of coefficient of determination remains the same.

Conclusion

The low level of per capita commercial energy consumption characterizes developing countries like Nepal. Developing countries are facing a great challenge of environmental degradation, deforestation, desertification, poverty alleviation, poor health of the people, unfavourable balance of payment and low economic growth. These issues are directly or indirectly related to energy use, availability and pattern of its consumption. Today developing countries make various efforts to overcome these issues. The income of a country has the close and positive relationship with energy consumption. Energy security, and conservation for achieving high economic growth is one of the most important function of developing countries. How much energy is needed to achieve specified economic growth and what is the role of energy in changing lifestyle of people are the major concerns in modern era. To answer these questions, quantitative forecasting of energy requirement is needed. Some of the widely used models of energy demand forecasting are presented and taking time series data of Nepalese economy also makes possible application of these models. Fuel wise income elasticity revealed that there is the high responsiveness of energy demand in Nepalese economy.

Environmental degradation, deforestation, desertification, poverty alleviation and health hazards of the people are the major concern of developing countries of the world today. These issues are directly or indirectly related to energy use and pattern of its consumption. In order to save our common earth which is depleting from one form to another (desertification, ecological imbalance etc.), protecting health hazards of people, reducing poverty, correcting balance of payment and providing better and efficient form of energy, energy development programmes, its security and conservation has become major concern to developing countries. These issues can be addressed by achieving high economic growth for which energy is one of the major ingredient or component to be developed. An essential factor of examining energy consumption pattern in developing countries, lifestyle of people, relationship between income and energy consumption, analysis of energy efficiency etc. is to forecast the energy demand in an economy. Wide research, comprehensive analysis of energy use, energy resource base etc. will provide the basis of energy demand forecasting. Here, an attempt is made to provide some basic tools to use when canalizing energy demand forecasting in developing countries. Trend analysis will provide the basis of energy demand forecasting. However, the developing countries are characterized by the lack of adequate and comprehensive data. So, the researchers should be aware of use this method to estimate energy demand.

1.3 DEVELOPING AND SELLING HYDROPOWER: NEPAL NEEDS TO REDUCE TARIFF*

Nepal possesses immense water resources as well as the best-suited topographical structure aiding the conduction and operation of a huge number of hydro-electric projects varying in capacity. The first hydro-electric project in Nepal installed at Pharping in 1911 had a generating capacity of 500 kW. However, the development of hydropower received higher priority only during the sixties. China and Nepal started to install hydro-electric plants at around the same time. China is one of the largest producer of hydro-electricity today with a per capita electricity generation and per capita electricity consumption of 988kWh and 934kWh respectively in 1999, compared to 56kWh and 47kWh in Nepal.

The recent installation of the 144 MW Kali-Gandaki 'A' has increased Nepal's total hydropower generation to 450 MW. This figure represents 0.3 per cent of the total theoretical and 1.07 per cent of economically feasible potential.

Efforts were started during that period to develop the Karnali Hydro-electric project until it was dropped in late 1980s for lack of sufficient foreign aid. The government then made efforts to harness the 402 MW Arun III hydro-electric project. Finance again became the major issue for the

---

* Published in The Himalayan Times, October 2, 2002.

implementation of Nepal's possibly largest power project. This project primarily initiated by World Bank was dragged into long debates among Nepalese intellectuals and politicians. As a result of this, the World Bank turned down the proposed Arun III hydro-electric project in 1995. With World Bank, help a highly controversial Pancheswar hydro-electric project alternatively named as the Mahakali integrated project was initiated. This more controversial project created a dissent among the existing political parties of the country. Despite disagreements among the lawmakers and public controversy, a treaty with the Indian Government over this project was signed in 1996.

Initiation to Private Sector

It has been felt that private sector has an important role to play in the development of hydropower. Thus, since the Eighth Five Year Plan (1992), the government decided to initiate private sector participation in harnessing the vast hydropower potential of the country. Consequently, the government formulated Water Resources Act in 1992 and implemented it. However, the Water Resources Strategy to adequately address the issue of "encouraging private investment in hydropower" was not succesful.

In spite of the poor implementation of the Act, two hydro-electric projects namely Khimti and Bhote Koshi were constructed and are running successfully under private sector investment. There is much duplication concerning the role of private sector involvement in exploiting hydro-electricity. There is a need to amend and update the existing Water Resources Act to highlight the new policy thrust on private sector outlined in the strategy. A clear and favourable Act is needed to attract foreign governments, multinational international companies and national institutions and individuals to invest in the development of hydro-electricity. Private sector involvement in harnessing hydropower potential would be effective only when the process of participation in the generation of electricity is transparent.

Electricity Consumption

Electricity consumption is an indicator of economic development of a country. Lower level of consumption of electricity as commercial energy indicates lower level of economic development of the country and vice-versa. Generally, per capita electricity consumption is used to measure living standard of the people of a country. Nepal's per capita electricity consumption is one of the lowest in the world. A recent study shows that 14 per cent of the total population of Nepal has access to electricity and most of the electricity facility is concentrated in the urban areas. The per capita electricity consumption of Nepal was 47 kWh in 1998, the lowest among selected developing Asian countries (Bhutan 600 kWh, Bangladesh 81 kWh, Myanmar 60 kWh, Pakistan 337 kWh, China 934 kWh, Maldives 220 kWh, and India 443 kWh).

Hydropower Market

South Asia is an energy-starved region of the world. Majority of its population needs electrical energy to supplement the use of traditional energy. India and Bangladesh are in urgent need of electricity in order to make up for the power shortage in the near future. Nepal's immediate neighbouring country India is estimated to require electricity amounting to 111500 MW between now and 2017. This provides ample market for the electricity generated in Nepal. However, Nepal is not a single country as the producer of hydro-electric power in the region. Bhutan too is producing huge quantity of electricity. The receipt from the sale of electricity covers half of the national budget of Bhutan. Bhutan embarked on developing electricity in the early eighties, two decades after Nepal did. This fact gives us a lesson that Nepal's ample potentiality of hydro-electricity seeks war-footed development efforts. The socio-economic condition of the Nepalese can be greatly improved if the country is able to harness electricity from its vast unused water resources. The electricity cost in Nepal is one of the highest in the world. It amounts to Rs. 10 per unit of electricity. To make Indian market accessible, Nepal should revise its electricity tariff rate because Bhutan sells electricity to India at the rate of Rs. 1.7 per unit of electricity. Similarly, Bhutanese government provides electricity facility to its citizens at the reasonable rate for domestic consumption as compared to the rate of a unit of electricity charged for the domestic consumption in Nepal. The tariff is a maximum of 80 Paisa per unit of electricity for urban consumers in Bhutan. Therefore, without reducing the power tariff Nepal does not have a good opportunity to expand its sale of electricity to Indian market. However, the northern states of India close to the Nepal border are facing an acute power shortage. Out of India's total shortfall in power they need about 14000 MW of electricity. This offers a ready market for Nepal.

This can be duly attributed to the lack of commitment the government has shown to hydropower. The policies are hazy and their implementation inefficient and these are multiplied by the country's insufficient funds to undertake a project by its own, the direct consequence of which is that 86 per cent of the population is unaware of what electricity is.

1.4 PATTERN OF ENERGY CONSUMPTION IN NEPAL*

The concept of energy has become more popular since the first energy supply shock of 1973, because in the end of 1973, the announcement and subsequent implementation of the Arab oil embargo stunned the world. After this announcement the price of petroleum products raised substantially by the OPEC countries so that the rest of the world started seeking for the development of reliable alternative energy sources. For this reason, energy is said to be the issue of this modern era. It has become the subject of debate in the global perspective. Although energy was used in pre-historic times, until the 18th century, almost all energy was supplied locally from such traditional sources as human and animal power, wood, dung,

---

* *Modified from the original paper published in VIKAS, A Journal of Development, Vol.18, No. 2, 1999, pp.42-55.*

crop residues, charcoal peat and utilization of wind and water power. As time passed by, there was substantial reform in health sector so that there was massive growth of population in the world, increase in the desire of comfort, material, acquisition, mobility and communication and access to the materials processes and technology to meet such desires by an increasing number has brought it among other things, rising energy demand incentive to meet that demand.

The British physicist Thomas Young defined energy, as 'energy is the capacity to do work'. This definition applied in the early 19th century to mechanical energy is still valid today. What people seek from energy use are the services energy provides such as heating, cooling, cooking, lighting and motive power. Energy is not a mere commodity to other human requirements or concern. The provision and use of energy wether efficiently and above all wether they have the means to use it.

Nepalese Context

From the earlier period to date, Nepal is dependent on the traditional source of energy consumption. With the decline in infant mortality, increase in average life expectancy and improvement in sanitation and health care are the result of industrialization process advanced.

Admittedly, this provides the goods and services required in part to sustain the population growth and eventually provided the technology to mitigate many of the problems it had caused. But in this context, Nepal has the alarming rate of growth of population, without development in other sectors, to mitigate the problems the population growth had caused. Higher the level of energy consumption, better will be the well-being of people of a country. In other words, energy consumption reflects the development and advancement of human beings. So it is one of the measuring parameter of the development of a country.

Among the commercial sources, Nepal has immense capacity to generate hydro-electric power as an alternative source of energy. Other sources of commercial energy are scarce within the country, these are being supplied from imports. Imports of such commercial energy largely depend on the foreign exchange reserves on the one hand and intensity of consumption on the other. Nepal has the potential hydropower of 83 thousand MW. Having this potential of hydropower, it has not been able to serve one per cent of total energy consumption in Nepal. If this resources of energy can be harnessed and utilized the traditional pattern of energy consumption can easily be supplemented from the development of this immense and valuable source of energy. The per capita energy consumption in Nepal is much lower than the average energy consumption of the world and even it is low when compared to nations of the SAARC. As a consequence of low development of commercial energy the bulk of energy requirements are met by fuel wood so that there is massive deforestation causing adverse environmental impacts. Similarly, the use of animal residues as fuel reduces the availability of organic fertilizer and increase the use of chemical fertilizer which adversely affects soil, drinking water, fishery and livestock.

Energy policy of His Majesty's Government

In the last eight periodic plans hydro-electric energy has been considered as one of the main infrastructure required for the economic development of the country. Consequently a huge amount of money was spent in the development of hydropower generation as a source of alternative energy requirements. It was mentioned in the sixth plan document that small hydro plants would be developed as an alternative energy to fuel wood. Besides this, the proposed small hydro-electric projects are located mostly in the district head quarters. Now-a-days, the new concept, which has been publicized so much, is that the hydropower in Nepal would be useful for the neighboring countries, that means the electric energy generated from the big Mega power stations would reach beyond the border of Nepal. From the above point of view the government has had dual policy of developing hydropower through state as well as private sectors.

The possibility of participation of private capital was supposed in the early sixties and this was continued in the budget speech of the FY 1984-85, which states that " If power generation plants of 100 KW capacity come up in the private sector the HMG will buy power from such undertakings. Similar policies were adopted by the government after the restoration of multi-party system in 1990. Taking this policy as guideline the eighth five year plan (1992-97) clearly states that 'No licenses will be required for the hydro-electric projects with up to 100 KW capacity. Besides this, there are various policies to facilitate the private investors in order to harness the available water resources of the country. Joint venture from the national and foreigners were expected to come in the development of hydro-electric power projects generation during the plan period. Besides the policy of harnessing hydro-electric power the Eight five-year plan had taken various policies to fulfill the growing energy demand in the country. Programs like the users group in order to maintain continuity in the supply of traditional energy and the policy to encourage private sector in the afforestation programs by making available forestland on lease. Likewise, promotion of renewable energy technologies would be encouraged in order to reduce the current dependence of traditional and imported fuels. Similar policies are adopted in the basic approach paper to Ninth plan (1997-2002)

Energy Pattern

Nepal is only an agriculture society with nine-tenths of its population in rural area and nearly a half of its GDP originates from this sector. In Nepal food crisis follows rapid population growth because of the low productivity of agriculture that depends so largely on human and animal energy. As a consequence, more than 60 per cent of the population resides below the poverty line. Starvation, malnourishment and famines are considered as the anti-social evils for the development and advancement of human resource prosperity in Nepal. Table 1.10 shows the energy consumption pattern in Nepal.

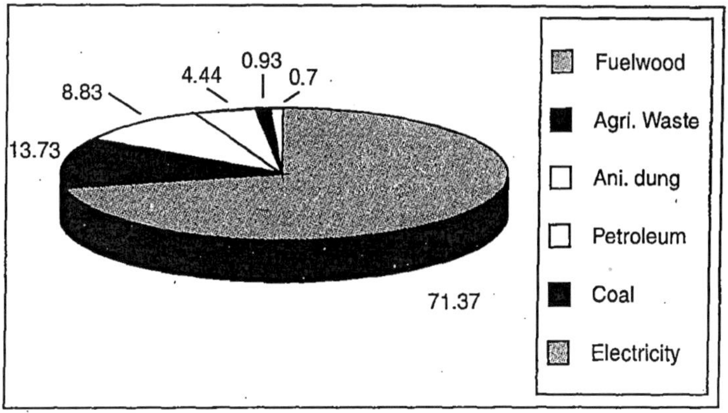

Fig.1.7 Share of Total Energy Consumption in Nepal

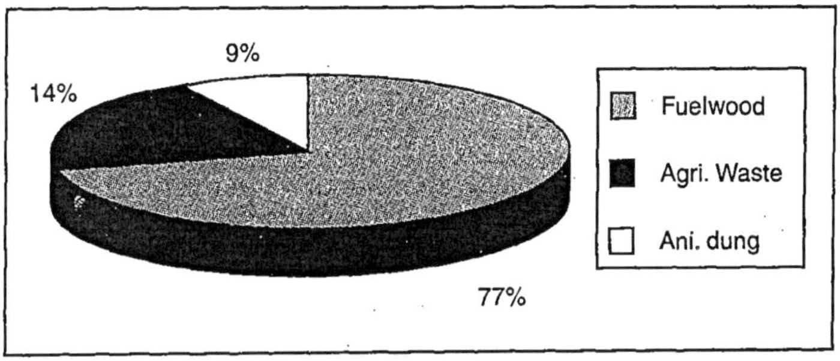

Fig.1.8 Share of Traditional Energy Consumption in Nepal

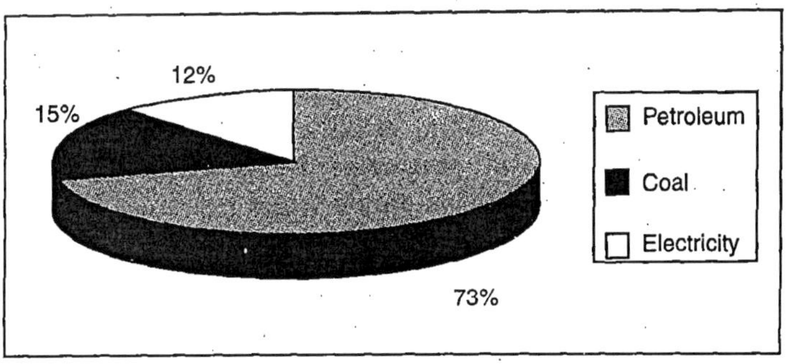

Fig.1.9 : Share of commercial Energy Consumption in Nepal

TABLE 1.10
Pattern of Energy Consumption

	Particulars	Per cent	Annual growth rate
1	**Traditional**	–	–
	(a) Fuelwood	71.37	2.1
	(b) Agriculture waste	13.73	3.6
	(c) Animal dung	8.83	1.1
	Total	93.93	2.3
2	**Commercial**	–	–
	(a) Petroleum products	4.44	8.83
	(b) Coal	0.93	2.4
	(c) Electricity	0.70	10.2
	Total	6.07	7.3
	Total 1+2	100	2.5

Source: Economic Survey FY 1995/96. MOF/HMG.

The annual growth rates are calculated by using the compound interest rate formula.

$S = Po\,(1+i)^t$ *where* $t = 16$.

The above table reveals that about 94 per cent of the total energy requirement in Nepal is supplied by non-commercial sources. The energy consumption is 78 per cent. As stated above more than 90 per cent of the population resides in the rural areas where the sources of energy requirements are met by traditional sources. As a result, massive deforestation has been taking place causing adverse affect on environment. Among the transitional sources the fuel wood, agricultural waste and animal residue occupy 77, 14 and 9 per cent share respectively to meet the growing demand of energy consumption in Nepal. In this regard, the Economic Survey, 1995/96 states that 'Nepal ranks among the world's top hydropower potential countries. Despite this potential, success in the utilization of ample water resources has been negligible. On the one hand large sum of money is being spent on the import of petroleum products and coal etc. in order to meet the ever-growing demand while on the other hand Nepal's limited forest resources are gradually depleting due to excessive dependence on this traditional energy source. The annual growth rate of traditional source of energy is 2.3, which is at par with the growth rate of population, followed by 2.1, 3.6 and 1.1 annual growth rates of fuelwood, agricultural waste and animal dung during 1980/81–1995/96 respectively.

Nepal Living Standard survey 1996 reveals that the main energy source for cooking is firewood. 68 per cent of the households are covered by this source as the main source of energy consumption, followed by animal dung and agriculture waste, kerosene and other sources which occupy 26, 1.4 and 1 per cent respectively. Firewood and animal dung are the main fuels used for cooking in all quintiles—all rich and poor households. In the urban areas, especially in Kathmandu valley, LPG is used by less than one per cent of total urban households. Whereso kerosene is used for cooking in urban centers of Nepal where 5 per cent of wealthier households use it. Inhabitants of rural areas are using Kerosene as the primary sources of energy. The rest of the households in rural areas are using Kerosene for the lighting purposes only. The southern part of the country, which is called as Tarai Region, is badly affected by massive deforestation. This is due to the fact that there is an increment of heavy population pressure inside as well as outside migration. As a result of this massive deforestation, the primary source of energy in this region is covered by the animal dung and agriculture waste. In some parts of this region, there is a scarcity of forest resources. This creates the compulsion for the communities to use animal dung and agriculture waste in order to meet their primary energy requirements.

Commercial Energy

Turning to the commercial energy, Nepal does not have any proven reserves of fossil fuel till now. Coal, petroleum products and electricity constitute the main commercial forms of energy used.

There is no possibility of extracting POL products in Nepal. The consumption of POL products is incrcasing due to the extension of roads, increase in the modern transport vehicles etc. The bulk of demand of this source of energy is being met by imports. These imported POL products are used primarily in the transport sector and to some extent in the domestic sector and account for about 4.4 per cent of the total energy consumption. Due to unavailability of this source of energy inside the country the whole POL products requirement of the country have to be imported so that a substantial amount of foreign exchange is spent for this purpose. The ratio of the expenditure on POL products import to GDP during the FY 1993/94–1995/96 is 0.02. It means 2 per cent of GDP has been spent on the import of POL products in Nepal. Among the commercial energy sources, POL products alone fulfill the bulk of growing energy demand. About 73 per cent of commercial energy consumption was met by this source during the period 1980/81–1995/96.

This alarming dependence on POL products in Nepal calls for the innovation and development of alternative sources of commercial energy on the one hand and there are millions of rupees in deficit with respect to its foreign trade on the other. The balance may be met in foreign trade if our immense water resources can be utilized to meet the bulk of growing energy requirements in Nepal. The development of these resources, not only brings balance between foreign trade but also it reduces the excessive dependence on traditional energy and preserve the environmental degradation by supplementing the use of fuel wood as primary energy.

The annual growth rate of POL products is high i.e. 8.3 per cent during period of 1980/81–1995/96. This growth rate calls for more import of this source of energy because of increase in the number of modern vehicles in the government as well as in the private sector.

Another imported commercial energy used in Nepal is coal. Mostly the coal is being used in the industrial sector. There are no adequate reserves of coal in Nepal. Thus the requirement of coal is met by imports. The consumption of coal in the total energy consumption is less than one per cent during the same period of time. The annual growth rate of coal is 2.4 per cent.

Electricity

Among the endowment of natural resources in Nepal the most important and adequate natural resource is water. The endowment of these water resources is an important factor in determining the present state of its economy and potential for future development. Nepal's endowment of many other important resources (land, forest, petroleum Products, minerals etc.) other than water resources is very poor. Of the various forms of energy, electricity is particularly important in the context of Nepal. The provision of electricity can greatly enhance the quality of life in Nepal, particularly of the poor. It provides health standards and assists in education and motivating people. Rural electrification also helps to enhance opportunities for income generation and employment in rural areas. The extent that it displaces less efficient and more environmentally damaging fuels and the country will adequately be benefited through the sale of electricity within the SAARC region, particularly to India. Electricity is essential for the sustainable development. Having these multipurpose objectives of electricity there is an urgent need to harness hydropower in Nepal.

The present contribution of electricity in total energy consumption is not satisfactory. The annual growth of electricity is 10.2 per cent. It contributed only 0.70 per cent in the total energy consumption during the period of 1980/81– 1995/96. Besides it provides 12 per cent of total commercial energy consumption during the same period.

"The water is a free good, it possesses no owner or price, developers of this new energy resources use it without paying for it and thereby pass the actual cost on to society" (*Marcus: 1992*).

Future Trends

The reality is that in the present Nepal, 90 per cent of the population do not have access to commercial energy and services it brings. This is a principally accepted view that the great majority of the people of Nepal have no energy other than muscle power, perhaps few domestic animals and traditional fuels, increasingly difficult to obtain in the desired quantity. What brings this difficulty in obtaining energy requirements? It is the question, which has the single answer that the high rate of population growth has brought forward the cultivation of marginal forest land on a massive scale. The forest and pasture land becoming scarce day-by-day. As a result, there is massive deforestation due to increase in the population pressure. 60 per cent of population resides below the poverty line. They do not even have access to food for their livelihood. In such a situation, the people who live under poverty line do not use adequate energy requirements. The country still is dependent on the traditional source of energy, which is obtained from the forest, agriculture waste and animal dung. Only 10 per cent of the population particularly the urban residents, have the access to commercial energy. Kerosene is used on a massive scale in order to cook the food in urban centers of Nepal.

The access to fuelwood as the primary source of energy consumption has the adverse affects on environmental impacts such as soil erosion, decrease in the fertility of arable land and increases the imbalance in the ecology within the universe. This also has the affects on human wealth that prevents the human resources development. Owned this property of the consumption of these resources, fuelwood used in the country is highest among the traditional source of energy. It occupied 77 per cent of the traditional sources of total energy consumption followed by 10 and 9 per cent by the agricultural waste and animal dung respectively during the period of 1980/81–1995/96. This excess dependency on traditional sources of energy consumption will continue in the future where the development of commercial energy is at stake.

The annual growth rate of energy consumption in Nepal is 2.5 per cent during the above stated period. The rate of growth of energy consumption is neck-to-neck with the population growth rate of 2.3 per cent per annum. This rate of growth of population and energy consumption requirements for the next 10 years will be 9133 thousand

TABLE 1.11
Estimated Energy Requirement after 10 Years (1995/96–2004/05)

	Heading	*Estimated energy requirement (in Thousand TOE)*
1.	**Traditional sources**	7898
	(a) Fuelwood	5793
	(b) Agriculture Waste	1491
	(c) Animal dung	614
2.	**Commercial Sources**	1235
	(a) POL products	934
	(b) Coal	91
	(c) Electricity	210
3.	Total 1+2	9133

Source: Estimated by the author taking the base period data of the FY 1995/96.

TOE. Thus, this excessive reliance on fuelwood as the primary energy requirement is going to pose further environmental problems and calls for a strategy of:

(a) increasing the productive capacity of the resources through better management of forests and afforestation program,
(b) conserving fuelwood through wide dissemination of improved cooking stoves, and
(c) substituting other energy forms such as biogas for fuel wood.

This strategy is affected in the master plan of forestry sector 1986- 2011, which is now under implementation.

Now, turning to the commercial energy, the consumption of POL products and coal is increasing in Nepal recently. The annual growth rate of POL products as stated above is 8.3 per cent and it covers the highest percentage of total commercial energy consumption in Nepal. This is not because of the expansion of industrial sector but because of the increasing number of modern transport vehicles. In order to reduce the excessive reliance on POL products, which is not the native source of energy, calls for the strategy of:

(a) reducing the number of modern transport vehicles in government and private sector as well,
(b) supplementing this reduction of means of transport system in the country, and
(c) promoting and developing the trolley bus system on the east-west highway.

If the remedial measures to reduce these are not taken early, its import will double after 10 years reaching 9133 thousand TOE. It will require a large amount of foreign exchange reserves thereby increasing the trade deficit of the country.

Among the commercial sources of energy, the native source of energy in Nepal is electricity. Nepal's long-term objective is to develop its enormous hydro-electric power resources both for domestic use and for export, thereby increasing its export earning to finance overall of its economic development. There are two thoughts for the development of hydro-power. *Firstly*, the mini hydel projects are to be launched in order to provide access to electricity to the rural people of the country. This strategy was overlooked in the past and is still valid today. The development of such projects may expand the small scale industries in the periphery on the one hand and on the other hand dependence of energy consumption on fuelwood will be supplemented by electricity, thereby preserving forest resources in order to prevent further environmental degradation. The *second* thought, which is publicized recently is that the construction of high or large dams will generate adequate electricity for domestic consumption as well as for export. The export earnings will therefore be the basis of further development of the country. Some thought provokes that the excess electricity of Nepal will be consumed by India if the comparative cost of electricity produced in Nepal is lower. In this respect Nepal could not attract foreign investment in this sector and there is a dilemma to invest in Nepal's electricity development by the bilateral and multilateral donors.

The consumption of electricity will increase three-fold

after 10 years with the annual growth rate of 10.2 per cent. The total quantity will reach 210 thousand KW. This rate of increase in electricity consumption requires that the existing capacity must rise three-fold after 10 years. Therefore, it is necessary to make war-footed efforts to generate additional hydro-electric power by mobilizing domestic as well as foreign capital. In order to meet this requirement the small, medium and large projects are to be launched simultaneously which are the basis of access to electricity to the entire population of the country and thereby increase export earnings which reduce the large deficit in foreign trade of Nepal.

Conclusion

Nepal's use of energy has been increasing very rapidly not because of the growth rate of industries but because of the alarming population growth. Energy demand is closely related to GDP not only in manufacturing, construction but also on farming, food processing and goods distribution. Therefore, the general objectives of energy policy are for the program to support national economic development by increasing energy production in accordance with the needs for balanced economic growth. To achieve this goal of energy policy, it is necessary to rationalize the production and consumption of energy thereby diversifying the use of new renewable sources of energy. If the existing pattern of energy consumption is continued, Nepal may face the challenge of environmental degradation that raises the adverse affects in agricultural productivity and human resource development. The above stated objective of economy can be achieved through reduction of large proportion of primary POL products in total imports. Conserving the forest resources and their gradual substitution by hydro-electric power should be considered as a basic requirement of energy policy in the years to come. Energy crisis of the 70s has had serious effect on the economies of the world for the reason that in 1973 the OPEC announcement and subsequent implementation of the oil embargo stunned the world. So, energy crisis has deeply been felt seriously by the developed as well as under-developed countries of the world. As a consequence various sources of alternative energy had been developed and the operation and implementation of such technology speeds up throughout the world. However, despite advanced technology with respect to energy, Nepal is virtually dependant on traditional source of energy consumption. Above 94 per cent of the energy consumption in Nepal is covered by this source. The sample potential of hydro-electric power, as a commercial source of energy, has not yet been able to contribute even one per cent of the total energy consumption. The POL products meet the commercial energy demand and the forest resources of Nepal cover the major part of the traditional energy demand.

1.5 MAHAKALI TREATY: IS IT GOING TO BE A CURSE?

For some time a debate has been taking place in Nepal (and also in India) about utilization of the Mahakali River bordering Nepal with India. Without seeking any prior formal consent from Nepal, India started to construct a dam on the Mahakali River at Tanakpur before one and half decade ago. The first elected government of Nepal headed by Girija Prasad Koirala of the Nepali Congress Party signed a treaty with India regarding the construction of Tanakpur barrage at the Mahakali River.

But that treaty was destined to become one of the most controversial chapters in Nepal's history. Regarding the process of its ratification, the Supreme Court of Nepal had to pass a verdict.

The court ruled that a treaty, such as the Tanakpur barrage one, the concerned parties should know that the development and distribution of natural resources must be ratified by the parliament, meaning that it was to be passed by a two-third majority of the legislators. Thus, the court transferred the responsibility of resolving the treaty of Tanakpur barrage to the Nepalese Parliament.

---

* Published in Everest Herald, Sept. 16, 1996.

Following the defeat of the Nepalese Congress Party in the 1994 mid-term polls, the minority government of the Communist Party of Nepal (UML), formed after the elections, proposed concepts of "Integrated Mahakali Development Project" during its short tenure in the office. As a result of its efforts the coalition government has signed a treaty with India in order to solve the problem of the Sharda Tanakpur and Pancheswar barrages.

But as it was signed without adequate homework in Nepal, the treaty still contains many provisions with serious implications, which do not guarantee Nepal her due rights in certain counts.

A concept should be made that we, by selling water to India, can use Nepal's water as a market in exchange of commodities and it can be the main source for Nepal's income generation.

But the so-called intellectuals and water resource specialists here haven't been able to take it seriously due to lack of a clear concept about water resource development. Our experts still believe that water resource development means only generating and selling electricity. Yes, generating electricity and selling it is certainly a development of water resources, but it is not the only way of doing so.

Agriculture is the base of survival for human beings in the present world, and every country is trying its best to develop agriculture. For the development of agriculture and production of more crops, water for irrigation is essential. Thus, for the development of agriculture, there is no alternative to it than water itself. But electricity can be generated by various means and methods. Therefore, it can be said that the development of agriculture by irrigating the land areas and producing more crops is an optimum form of water resources development.

India has planned to irrigate 113 million hectares of its land before 2005. For irrigation of such a vast area of land, India does not have sufficient water.

Even the water it has is difficult for it to transport from one place to another due to topographical structure of its geography. Therefore, it has to depend upon Nepal for water. In the name of electricity, which they are buying, they are going to get water of Nepal almost free of cost due to the foolishness of the so-called Nepali intellectuals and politicians.

Nepal, being a poor country as it is, has not been able to develop anything including water. About the development of water resources, Nepal has signed some treaties with India time and again. But it is seen that through the treaties Nepal just has only one motive – to sell electricity to India.

Electricity is not the thing which Nepal has been generating most either. Yes, Nepal is a country rich in water resources, though. But according to the master plan of India, it has been trying to get the required water from Nepal. In a country like Nepal, it is necessary to generate profit through water, which can be done only when water is used as a market commodity.

India is in great need of water for irrigation of a vast area of land. So, Nepal should be able to bargain with India to convince it to buy the water from Nepal. At present what India needs is water more than electricity. Nepal should be able to understand this strategic move of India and make the best development of her water resources by dealing accordingly. Taking the necessity of India into account, Nepal should endeavour to make water a market commodity and sell it to its neighbour.

The dams made on the border points between Nepal and India has created a great loss of the fertile lands of Nepal in the Terai plain. It also creates havoc to the settlements of Nepal close to the border because contructing dams, blocks the natural flow of water into India.

The Pancheshwar barrage will also create the same problem to Nepal in future. It is also a serious matter to be considered prior to the final rectification of the Mahakali Treaty in the Parliament. Before the consideration of above points, however, it is equally necessary to find a permanent solution to border disputes at Mechi and Mahakali both.

After dividing the water and electricity between Nepal and India equally, Nepal should be fully ensured that the excess electricity as well as water would be bought by India.

The parliamentarians should be able to understand the above points and include them in the Treaty, before rectifying it. But if these points are overlooked and the Treaty is ratified in the present form, it will be a very big loss, misfortune and even curse to Nepal.

1.6 ENERGY AND ECONOMY*

The level of economic development in the present world is largely determined by per capita energy consumption and hence this indicator shows the living standard of people. The World Bank estimates that Nepal's per capita GNP is equivalent to US$ 220 and 51 per cent of the total population lives under absolute poverty with an income less than one dollar a day. This is the scenario now Nepal is facing. The main source of energy in Nepal is biomass that accounts for over 90 per cent of the total energy consumption.

Fuelwood has always been the dominant source of energy in Nepal. It fulfills over 80 per cent of the primary energy requirement of the people. The major sources of fuelwood are public forests, shrub lands, grasslands and private holdings. The annual growth rate of fuelwood consumption during 1984/85–1994/95 was 2 per cent. Fuelwood is likely to remain the principal sources of energy in the foreseeable future. However, it is important to note that the depletion of forest is the major concerns of the recent times. The growing demand for firewood coupled with the mismanagement of its sources is exhausting the forest cover and resulting in

(*a*) increased usage of agricultural waste and the same of animal dung. These increased with a growth rate of 4.5 per cent and 1.3 per cent per annum during 1984/85–1994/95 respectively. Increased usage of animal dung as primary source of energy directly imposes

* Modified from the original paper published in Readings in Nepalese Economy, Nepal Society of Applied Economic Research, 2001, pp. 47-50.

adverse effect in agricultural productivity because it is used as a source of energy rather than a supplement to crop as fertilizer.

(b) environmental degradation through soil erosion, and
(c) increased wastage in gathering of firewood.

Forest resources, a major source of energy, has dwindled over time due to continuous extraction for domestic and commercial use. WECS has estimated a total forest and shrub land of 4520.94 thousand hectare of which 2127.81 thousand hectare is accessed for fuelwood collection. While making this estimation it has been assumed that the rate of depletion is 2 per cent per annum.

Energy is a commodity that fulfills human basic needs like cooking, heating and lighting. As stated above, the traditional source of energy plays dominant role in our society. In the fiscal year 2000/01 the share of traditional energy was 86 per cent of which 77 per cent accounted for fuelwood consumption followed by agricultural waste 3.5 per cent and animal dung 5.7 per cent. Only the remaining 14 per cent was accounted for commercial source. The contribution of coal, petroleum products and electricity is 2.8, 9.5 and 1.4 per cent respectively within the same period. Consumption of commercial energy has been considered to be an indicator of economic development which determines the level of economic development, life style of people, urbanization and industrialization.

TABLE 1.12
Consumption of Energy in Nepal

(in per cent)

Sources	*1998/99*	*1999/00*	*2000/01*
Traditional	87.9	87.1	86.4
Commercial	12.1	12.9	13.6

Source: Economic Survey, 2001.

The above table reveals that there is an increasing trend in consumption of commercial energy. The increasing trend in commercial energy is associated with the increasing trend of urbanization, expansion of road facilities, advancement of industrial development, modernization of agriculture and motivation towards service sector. However, Nepal has low level of commercial energy consumption. Nepal's Water and Energy Commission has estimated that per capita consumption of commercial energy is 15 GJ. Among the commercial sources of commercial energy consumption the highest proportion of it is attached to the consumption of petroleum products whose overall demand is met by import. The highly increasing consumption of POL products has an adverse effect on the country's balance of payment and balance of trade as well. The proportion of POL products during 1998/99–2000/01 is given below:

TABLE 1.13
Consumption of Commercial Energy

(in per cent)

Sources	*1998/99*	*1999/00*	*2000/01*
Coal	19.5	20.4	20.5
Petroleum	71.2	70.7	69.6
Electricity	9.3	8.9	9.9

Source: Economic Survey, 2001.

The consumption of petroleum in Nepal is the highest, which is followed by coal and electricity consumption respectively. The only indigenous source of energy, electricity contributes to about 9 per cent of the total commercial energy consumption, imported hydrocarbons fulfill the remaining 91 per cent. The total bill of petroleum import as per cent of merchandise export for 1998/99–2000/01 is given in table 1.14 below:

TABLE 1.14
Amount Paid to Import POL Products and PTL Imports as Per cent of Merchandise Export

Particulars	*1998/99*	*1999/00*	*2000/01*
Value (Rs. in million)	11136.1	13332.3	10335.9
POL imports as % of merchandise export	25.8	27.3	26.6

Source: Economic Survey, 2001.

The above table reveals that more than 26 per cent of the export earnings has been paid to the import of POL products in each fiscal year. The imported POL products particularly affect the balance of trade in our economy. The balance of trade during the same period is shown below:

TABLE 1.15
Balance of Trade of Nepal

(Rs. in million)

Particulars	*1998/99*	*1999/00*	*2000/01*
Export F.O.B	35676.3	51623.0	38900.0
Import C.I.F	87525.3	106966.8	75184.8
Trade Balance	–51849.0	–55343.8	–36284.8

Source: Economic Survey, 2001.

There is an increase in the use of POL products in Nepal, which has several effects. *Firstly,* there is a frequent change in the price of POL products in the world market. In such situation we have to bear a huge deficit in the balance of trade and divert our foreign exchange to import expensive petroleum products by minimizing development expenses. *Secondly,* the earning of our export trade cannot even meet import of the POL products. *Thirdly,* it gives rise to the consumption of luxury goods by the affluent people of our society. *Lastly,* it increases pollution and so on.

The uncontrolled use of imported petroleum products in Nepal should be reduced to a minimum, the substitution of imported fuel can only be made by the use of electricity. Nepal is a very rich country in water resources second only to Brazil. It would be very meaningful to generate hydro-electricity from the perpetual run of rivers. We can generate electricity and install plants ranging from one megawatt to thousands of megawatts throughout the country. Despite of this richness, Nepal is not able to utilize even one per cent of the total hydro-power potential. Even though Nepal is highly populated, only 14 per cent of its population has access to electricity, which contributes to only one per cent of the total energy consumption.

Realizing the commendable importance of hydro-electricity the Nepalese government has given top priority to utilize it as a source of alternative commercial energy to maximum extent. The government has allocated 18.43 per cent of the total development expenditure, which amounts to Rs. 9298.8 million for the development of electricity in the fiscal year 2001/02.

Huge projects such as Kaligandaki 'A' and middle Marshyangdi are provided with large budget of approximately around 60 per cent of the total allocated expenditure. It indicates that the development of small hydro-plants will be crowded out. So, the budget does not have a clear vision with respect to the development of small hydro-electric projects that provide energy to rural people of the country.

Presently the government has set an objective to generate hydro-electricity to the maximum extent by mobilizing internal and external resources. After the restoration of multi-party system in Nepal, the policy of the government has gone through several changes and generation of electricity by the private sector has been emphasized throughout.

1.7 RURAL DEVELOPMENT: PROMOTE RURAL ENERGY ACCESSIBILITY

People expect their lives to be improved with the turning of every year. They imagine, Nepal will become the congenial place to live in. The growing population pressure imposes serious threat on Nepal's stocks of natural resources particularly on the forests. Forest is a crucial renewable and perennial energy source, which covers more than 80 per cent of the energy requirement of Nepalese people and it is expected that it will continue to do so in the years to come. However, it is being depleted over time. Within five to ten years, if the present rate of forest depletion is allowed to continue, the demand for fuelwood will outstrip supply on the one hand and top soil of the farmland will be washed into the sea as a result of unsustainable farming on the other. The increasing pressure on natural resources and massive deforestation has led to unprecedented environmental degradation.

The expectation of everyone in Nepal is that the economic system will depend on never-ending growth. However, we are living today with finite resources on which the never-ending economic growth process depends. Thus, our expectation of progress results as a fantasy. There is no doubt that the rising population is one of the factors, which threatens Nepal's capacity to support its people. It is one of the factors for which the poor can be blamed and rich be excused although the consumption of affluent is supposed to be boundless.

With the expansion of an economy, the production of goods and services increases over time, which is the essential part of the pace of development. As production capacity of an economy increases, it requires more energy for sustaining the pace of development. In addition there are various factors that embody the increase in the consumption of energy. The accelerating and rapid development pace brings people to prosperous phase and their living standard improves as a result of which they require more energy for use in the household and in the industrial establishments. Rise in income of the people however, does not affect the energy demand for cooking. In contrast, the demand for energy will rise because of the use of modern appliances (radio, TV, refrigerator, freeze, washing machine, computer, transportation) with the rise in income. In the similar fashion, the rise in income of the people has direct and positive correlation in the process of urbanization, industrialization and agricultural modernization. The structural change in an economy needs commercial form of energy to sustain it. Thus, in this respect, it should be perceived that one has to pay attention to develop the energy related projects in the rural areas of the country in order to improve the lifestyle of the people and to increase the capability of the pace of development in a sustainable manner.

The twin objectives, sustainable development and poverty alleviation are the recent concerns of the governments of developing countries. These goals will be achieved only when the access to commercial energy in a sustainable manner is made available to the people of sparse and isolated villages of the country, which can safeguard and conserve non-renewable resources and forest in order to maintain the ecological balance.

The oil shock of 1970's threatened the world to maintain growing demand for commercial energy, particularly the petroleum products. Since then there has been a growing concern on the development of alternative renewable sources of energy as a result of which technological innovation has taken place beyond its limit.

Needless to say that Nepal has abundant untapped water resources. The generation of hydro-electricity has a slow development pace although it was started in 1911 with the installed capacity of 500 kW. Over the last nine decades the hydro-electricity generation has exceeded 450 MW. Today, electric energy has been served to only 14 per cent of the total population of the country and virtually remains in the urban centers of the country. This scenario ended up in a backward phase in providing electric energy to the people of villages where the main source of energy is fuelwood.

The growing concern today is forest depletion, which brings ecological imbalance and drives the country towards desertification. Thus, in this respect, unavailability of electric energy and injudicious use of resources have necessitated the formulation and implementation of rural energy development programmes to enhance rural energy development as well as preserve the environment through expansion and development of rural energy systems. The concerns over the development of rural energy were felt a few decades ago because of the expensive nature of the expansion of national electricity grid in the sparse and isolated villages of the country.

Keeping this in mind, the government is engaged in setting up a rural energy development basket fund for rural energy development. Donors, particularly Danish, German and Dutch governments and European Commission, back this fund. The aim of this fund among other things is to develop alternative renewable sources of energy in the rural areas in order to provide better energy services to the rural people, that is considered to be the prerequisite to promote and enhance the living standard of people and in turn conserve the deteriorating environment. The purpose of the basket fund is to develop and establish alternative renewable energy projects in the rural areas with a view to mobilize local resources to the maximum possible extent. If the fund is released for the purpose—at the right place and at the right time—is sufficient and prompt. This step will bring a crucial progress in the direction of rural energy development in the villages, which can change the lifestyle of people and safeguard the deteriorating environment. The development of rural energy is crucial in view of the rural development perspective in order to enhance the living standard of people and can bring natural resources into balance, a key factor for promoting economic growth, prevent sharply the environmental degradation.

Projects related to energy such as micro-hydro, biogas, solar and wind are the present form of alternative renewable energy resources. The development, installation and modernization of these energy related small projects in the sparse and remote villages would provide among other things, better energy services to the rural people. The development and installation of such projects need a small amount to be invested and most of which can be mobilized from the targeted/users groups. If the government enhances R&D in the context of feasibility study in the rural areas with the policy of decentralization, possibility of local resource mobilization range will widen on a greater scale. Efforts are being placed time and again to develop alternative renewable sources of energy in the rural areas under the integrated rural development programmes. However, achievements were not in progress, which could not provide incentive, encouragement and competition within the stakeholders and investors.

Thus, the government should come forward to develop

alternative energy, which can provide better energy services to the people and in turn mitigate the utmost goal of the poverty alleviation. Formulation and implementation of the energy plan at the national as well as the district and village level with comprehensive programmes and policies including the clear direction of local level resource mobilization by examining the willingness and ability to pay-of the local people, is needed for the effective implementation of the energy related projects at the village level. So, in this respect, the institutions involved in the development of energy related projects should have to focus their attention in carrying out the detailed study to develop comprehensive energy plan, which may help to take decisions to implement programmes and policies in order to meet the need of the people.

1.8 ENERGY SYSTEM : NEED FOR NEW MOMENTUM

Poverty alleviation and obtaining high economic growth rate are some of the major issues of modern era. The periodic plans of Nepal have addressed these issues one after the other. Development and modernizing aspect of these issues, among other things, bringing sustainability, ecological balance, improving life style of people, reducing poverty are closely related to energy availability and energy resource base. Poor energy resource base restricts the supply of adequate energy required by an economy. As a result, Nepal is facing acute power shortage due to poor energy resource base. Nepal has no proven source of hydro-carbon deposits. The increasing need of the hydrocarbons is met by import. The total amount paid to import hydrocarbons was Rs. 13332.3 million in the fiscal year 2000/01 and it accounts to 27.3 per cent of merchandise export. Hydro-electricity is the only indigenous source of commercial energy. Its development and generation remain slow despite of efforts been made to harness the potential to the maximum possible extent.

Socio-economic Development and Energy

Human beings on the earth, now-a-days seek a better life and an improved standard of living. These fundamental aspirations of the people are related to socio-economic development as well as economic growth rate. Socio-economic development is one of the means to achieve these goals. Poor performance of economy turns these goals into fallacies. Nepal is a poor country with the lowest performance of its economy (per capita GNP US $220). Recently, the National Planning Commission of Nepal has estimated that 38 per cent of population live below the line of poverty. This situation reflects the political unrest which Nepal is facing today. People are migrating from rural to urban areas in order to achieve their fundamental goals of better life and minimum-security level. This trend of migration is not confined within the country only, people are migrating towards industrialized countries of the world to seek better standard of life.

For the poor, a better life means satisfying basic human needs including excess to jobs, food, health services, education, housing and so on. In providing such facilities to the poor people, energy plays an important role, because energy is an ingredient of socio-economic development and economic growth. The objective of the energy system is to provide energy services to the people. Energy provides the basic fundamental services like cooking, heating and lighting. In addition, processing of products and transportation are possible only through the energy services. Considering such important role of energy services from the perspective of fulfilling human basic needs and economic development, the growth rate of economy is closely related to energy consumption.

The growth trend of commercial energy consumption is much higher than the growth trend of real GDP. However, the growth trend of total energy consumption is parallel to the growth trend of real GDP. The average growth rate of commercial energy consumption is three times greater than that of real GDP, which indicates that in achieving high economic growth rate in Nepal, a substantial amount of energy is needed.

TABLE 1.16
Growth Rate of GDP and Commercial Energy Consumption in Nepal

(in Per cent)

Year	Real GDP	Commercial Energy Consumption	Total Energy consumption
1996/97	4.77	23.3	3.9
1997/98	3.44	16.8	3.6
1998/99	4.47	12.8	3.3
1999/00	6.40	12.4	5.4
2000/01	5.80	8.4	3.1

Source: Economic survey, 2001.

Energy Situation in Nepal

Most dominant source of energy in Nepal is biomass. 86 per cent of the population resides in the rural areas of the country. The energy requirement of these people is fulfilled by the biomass energy sources. Fuelwood plays an important role in fulfilling energy requirements of people. The traditional source of energy accounted for 87 per cent of total energy consumption during the fiscal year 2000/01. Fuelwood has contributed 77.4 per cent of total energy consumption followed by 3.5 and 5.7 per cent of agricultural waste and animal dung respectively. It proves that the consumption of commercial energy is insignificant. Only 13 per cent of the commercial energy has accounted for commercial energy sources during the same period. 2.8, 9.5 and 1.4 per cent has accounted for coal, petroleum and electricity respectively. Table 1.17.

The annual average growth rate of total energy consumption during 1984/85–2000/01 was 2.9 per cent. Similarly, the growth rate of fuelwood, agricultural waste and animal dung consumption was 2.3, 2.4, and 2.3 respectively. The average annual growth rate of coal consumption, petroleum consumption and electricity consumption was 6.2, 10.6, and 10.8 per cent respectively. The high growth rate of commercial energy consumption reveals that there is an

TABLE1.17
Structure of Energy Consumption in Nepal

(in per cent)

Year	Fuel wood	Agri. Waste	Animal dung	Coal	Petroleum	Electricity
1996/97	80.6	3.6	5.9	1.0	7.8	1.0
1997/98	79.4	3.5	5.9	2.2	7.8	1.1
1998/99	78.5	3.5	5.8	2.4	8.6	1.1
1999/00	77.7	3.5	5.7	2.6	9.1	1.1
2000/01	77.4	3.5	5.7	2.8	9.5	1.4

Source: Economic Survey, 2001.

increasing demand of commercial energy sources in Nepal. Relatively high growth rate of commercial energy consumption has led to changes in the energy consumption pattern on the one hand and indicates growth in terms of higher income and urbanization on the other.

TABLE 1.18
Annual Growth Rate 1984/85–2000/01

(in per cent)

Fuel wood	Agri. Waste	Animal dung	Coal	Petroleum	Electricity
2.3	2.4	2.3	6.2	10.6	10.8

Nepal has low level of commercial energy consumption. The per capita commercial energy in 1996 was only about 28kgoe.This is one of the lowest per capita energy consumption as compared to other developing Asian countries. For instance, China, India, Bangladesh, Pakistan and Sri Lanka had per capita commercial energy consumption of 705k goe, 298kgoe, 75kgoe, 283kgoe and 137kgoe respectively during the same period (Table 1.19). Why has Nepal low level of commercial energy consumption as compared to other developing Asian countries? It is a surprising fact that Bangladesh has the same level of economic development with respect to per capita GNP. However, the per capita consumption of commercial energy is three times greater than that of Nepal. This indicates the low level of

TABLE 1.19
Energy Indicators

Country	*Per Capita Energy Consumption (kgoe)*			*Energy Intensity in GDP (toe/'000 1993 US$)*			*Net Oil Imports Dependency (%)*		
	1985	1990	1996	1985	1990	1996	1985	1990	1996
Bangladesh	43	55	75	0.24	0.21	0.25	36.0	29.9	28.9
China	513	551	705	1.68	1.37	0.99	–0.9	–4.0	1.8
India	174	226	298	0.74	0.79	0.93	12.6	13.2	20.1
Nepal	18	14	28	0.12	0.08	0.14	53.3	52.0	75.4
Pakistan	210	223	283	0.65	0.58	0.64	31.0	30.7	40.7
Sri Lanka	84	90	137	0.23	0.17	0.21	70.3	68.7	99.7
Maldives	114	141	394	0.19	0.17	0.37	–	–	–

Source: Key Indicators of Developing Asian and Pacific Countries, Vol. XXXI, ADB, 2000.

economic development of Nepal because per capita commercial energy consumption is one of the devices of the economic development, which reflects the low level of the standard of people.

Now, turning to the energy intensity, Nepal is characterized by low-level energy intensity. Nepal has the energy intensity in GDP Gtoe/000 1993 US$ and for the year 1996 was about 0.14 thousand toe (1993 US$). In contrast, the same for other developing Asian countries during the same period were 0.25, 0.99, 0.93, 0.64; 0.21 and 0.37 of Bangladesh, China, India, Pakistan, Sri Lanka and Maldives respectively. The use of commercial energy is either characterized by the low level of price or by the technological deficiency. The low level of price of commercial energy always tends to decrease the intensity of energy. Technological deficiency indicates the use of absolute energy consumption machineries.

Biomass Energy

Nepalese energy consumption is dominated by biomass energy, which contributes to over 85 per cent of the total energy consumption of Nepal. Over 86 per cent of population resides in the rural areas. Biomass resources meet the energy requirement of rural people. Biomass includes fuelwood, crop residues and animal dung. Forest resources contribute over 80 per cent of total energy consumption of Nepal. Forests of Nepal are only energy resource base of the people of rural areas to fulfill their primary energy requirements. However, the forest resources of Nepal are dwindling over time.

There are various reasons for the high rate of depletion of forest in Nepal.

Firstly, increasing numbers of people rely on agriculture for their livelihood. As a consequence, the arable man-land ratio is continuing to diminish. On the context, people started to expand agricultural land by encroaching forest land.

Secondly, the forest provides not only fuel for cooking and heating, it also provides fodder and wood for construction as well as furniture. Therefore, heavy pressure on forest is accounted and its depletion rate is much higher than Re-plantation rate. Table 1.20 shows the historical trend of the consumption of biomass energy.

Table 1.20 reveals that fuelwood, as a major source of energy has contributed to 89 per cent of total traditional energy consumption. Among the traditional sources of energy, crop residues and animal dung has contributed to 4 per cent and 7 per cent respectively. This trend reveals that energy requirement of people of Nepal is met by traditional sources of energy of which fuelwood has been playing important role in fulfilling the energy needs. It is expected that the forests will continue to fulfill energy requirements of the people in the foreseeable future.

Electric Energy

Nepal's first hydropower plant was installed at Pharping in 1911 with a capacity of 500kW. After a long gap in the development of hydropower, the second hydropower plant was installed at Sundarijal with a generating capacity of 640kW in 1934. The third hydropower plant was established with a capacity of 677kW in eastern Nepal. This was the scenario of hydro-electricity generation of the country before the first half of the 20th century. In 1951, the political change

TABLE 1.20
Biomass Consumption in Nepal

(in '000 GJ)

Year	FW	%	AW	%	AD	%	Total
1984/85	183908.5	89.3	8228.28	4.0	13785.6	6.7	205922.4
1985/86	187871.9	89.3	8400.6	4.0	14044.08	6.7	210316.6
1986/87	191964.5	89.3	8572.92	4.0	14345.64	6.7	214883
1987/88	196143.2	89.3	8788.32	4.0	14690.28	6.7	219621.8
1988/89	200408.2	89.3	8960.64	4.0	14991.84	6.7	224360.6
1989/90	204759.2	89.3	9176.04	4.0	15293.4	6.7	229228.7
1990/91	207473.3	89.3	9305.28	4.0	15638.04	6.7	232416.6
1991/92	213763	89.3	9563.76	4.0	15982.68	6.7	239309.4
1992/93	218372.5	89.3	9779.16	4.0	16327.32	6.7	244479
1993/94	223154.4	89.3	9994.56	4.0	16671.96	6.7	249820.9
1994/95	227979.4	89.3	10253.04	4.0	17016.6	6.7	255249
1995/96	232976.6	89.3	10468.44	4.0	17404.32	6.7	260849.4
1996/97	238017	89.3	10683.84	4.0	17748.96	6.7	266449.8
1997/98	243229.7	89.3	10942.32	4.0	18136.68	6.7	272308.7
1998/99	248528.5	89.3	11157.72	4.0	18524.4	6.7	278210.6
1999/00	259470.8	89.3	11717.76	4.0	19299.84	6.7	290488.4

Source: Economic Survey, MOF/HMG, 2001

took place and Nepal started to expand its relationship with other countries of the world. As a result a hydro-electric plant was established in Pokhara (Phewa lake) with a generating capacity of 1000kW under bilateral co-operation with India. The project started to supply electricity in 1967. A series of hydro-power plants have been established since then in order to meet the growing demand of electricity. The existing hydro-power plants are listed in table 1.21.

A possible alternative to substituting the use of all types of energy in Nepal is the development and generation of the electric energy resources. However, one of the essential features of energy development program based on electricity is that it is capital intensive. Huge amount is needed to undertake large hydro-electric plant projects. A poor country like Nepal alone is not able to generate hydro-electricity from large-scale hydropower projects.

TABLE 1.21
Existing Hydropower projects of Nepal (2000)

(Capacity in kW)

Panauti	2400	Doti	200	Bajura	200
Trisuli	24000	Phidim**	240	Bajhang**	200
Sunkosi	10050	Gorkhe***	64	Arughat	150
Gandak	15000	Jomsom**	240	Tatopani I&II	2000
Kulekhani I	60000	Jumla**	200	Okhaldhunga**	125
Devighat	14100	Dhading***	32	Rupalghad	100
Kulekhni II	32000	Syangja***	80	Surnaiyagad	200
Marsyangdi	75000	Seti Pokhara	1500	Namche*	600
Aandhi Khola	51000	Helambu	50	Achham	400
Jhimruk	12300	Salleri	400	Kalikot	500
Chatara	3200	Darchula I&II**	300	Dolpa	200
Puwa Khola	6200	Chame	45	Mahendra (diesel)	1728
Khimti Khola	60000	Taplejung**	125	Biratnagar (diesel)	1028
Pharping***	500	Manang	80	Hetauda (diesel)	12750
Sundarijal	640	Chaurjhari**	150	Marsyangdi (diesel)	2250
Pehwa	1088	Syarpudaha**	200	Duhabi Multi-fuel I (diesel)	26000
Phankuta	240	Khandbari**	250	Duhabi Multi-fuel II (diesel)	13000
Tinau	1024	Terhathum**	100	Simikot (Solar)	50
Jhupra	345	Bhojpur**	250	Gamgadhi (Solar)	50
Baglung	200	Ramechhap	150	Grand Total	389574

Source: NEA at a Glance 1999/00.
Note : * Private and others
** Leased to the private sector
*** Not in normal operation

Inspite of these, given constraints, electricity has immense importance in the economic development of Nepal. Electric energy can play an important role in the development of national economy. Nepal is rich in water resources. It can generate electricity ranging from one MW to thousands of MW through its run of rivers. However, unfortunately, electric energy has contributed only to a meager 1.4 per cent of the total energy consumption during 2000/01 (Table 1.23). The supply side of electric energy is very weak because Nepal has not yet been able to generate even 1 per cent of electricity through its total hydro-electric potential.

Electricity is considered as the safest and cleanest source of energy. It has no contribution to environmental pollution. Nepal is facing air-pollution from the use of imported hydrocarbons as energy. The use of imported hydrocarbons can be substituted by electric energy to the maximum possible extent.

The generation of electricity has multifold advantages for the Nepalese economy.

First, it has no environmental pollution. Here it is important to note that Nepal is now facing environmental pollution through the use of hydrocarbons as a source of commercial energy.

Secondly, the use of hydrocarbons can be substituted by the electric energy and in turn it can save foreign currency, and

Thirdly, the generated excess quantity of electric energy can be exported to neighboring countries.

In addition, the high per capita consumption of electric energy is considered as the indicator of economic development.

TABLE 1.22

National Power Scene at a Glance

Description	*Unit*	*Existing Capacity (2000)*
Total Installed Capacity	MW	389.574
Hydro	MW	332.718
Diesel	MW	56.756
Solar	MW	0.100

Source: NEA, At A Glance, 2000, Kathmandu.

Considering the immense importance of electricity there is an urgent need to exploit water resources of the country. At present, Nepal has low level of per capita electricity consumption. The per capita electricity consumption in 1999 was only about 47 kWh. In contrast in period Bangladesh had 89kWh. The per capita energy consumption is also low as compared to other developing countries of Asia. Nepal has electricity intensity in GDP during the same period it was 0.22 kWh/'0001993 US $. The efficiency of electricity in GDP is also low as compared to other developing Asian countries under consideration. The electricity intensity was slightly higher than that of Maldives. Annex. 1 Table 6 shows that the electricity intensity of Bangladesh, Pakistan, Sri Lanka, and Maldives were 0.27, 0.74, 0.34, and 0.19 respectively in the same period.

There is great scope for future improvement in energy efficiency in Nepal. Presently, Nepal does not employ much of the existing technology to its full potential in raising the efficiency in energy provision and use. The full utilization of existing technology is primarily attributed to the failure of better management and better training. "Technical improvement has the ability to tackle inefficiency and control pollution because of their ability to utilize key economic factors, especially capital and technology coupled with relative openness informed quality of public debate" *(WEC, 1993:110)*

The Nature of the Problem

Despite abundant resources poured into the power sector, Nepal still faces huge shortage of power. Occurrence of frequent load shedding has become a daily phenomenon in Nepalese economy. It shows that Nepal faces an acute problem of power shortages. Bringing additional generation of power to meet the growing demand, huge investment is needed. Up-till now, major investment has been made by public sector during the five-year plans. However, the eighth plan (1992-97) has realized that public sector investment alone could not generate additional power to meet the growing demand. So the Government has changed to the policy of activating private sector finances in order to generate additional power in Nepal.

TABLE 1.23
Electricity Indicators

	Per Capita Electricity Generation (kWh)			*Per Capita Electricity Consumption (kW)*				*Electricity Intensity (kWh/000 1993*		
6	*1997*	*1998*	*1999*	*1996*	*1997*	*1998*	*1999*	*1996*	*1997*	*1998*
9	90	97	100	74	76	81	89	0.26	0.25	0.25
7	924	939	988	884	917	934	–	1.25	1.30	1.37
1	442	462	487	443	443	–	–	1.32	1.29	–
7	57	53	56	41	44	45	47	0.20	0.21	0.22
4	460	472	486	333	333	337	320	0.76	0.77	0.79
7	277	303	325	204	218	241	253	0.31	0.32	0.34
9	313	347	385	187	201	220	234	0.18	0.18	0.19

ors of Developing Asian and Pacific Countries, Vol. XXXI, ADB, 2000.

Nepal faces two main problems in generating additional electricity.

In the *first* place, Nepal Electricity Authority (NEA), which is considered as the sole producer and distributor, is financially sick. As a result NEA is not able to make huge investments in generating additional electricity as per the requirements of the country. In the second place, there is the lack of adequate trained manpower (experts) to undertake power generation projects independently. Having such problems, the generation of additional electricity mainly depends upon the foreign investments and expertise. Foreign finances in power sector, among other things primarily depend upon the demand for energy (market base) and price of the power to be generated in future and the purchasing power capacity of the government.

What Are The Possible Solutions?

Enhancing Private Sector participation

The government of Nepal has shifted to the policy of encouraging private sector participation in the generation of power onwards from eighth five-year plan (1992-97). This policy of encouraging private sector participation in production of energy is primarily aimed to fulfill the generation gap of electricity in the country. The government has taken the important decision to encourage private investment—both domestic and foreign—in electricity generation. The Ministry of Water Resources has brought forward some policy issues in order to attract foreign investments in generating electricity. Accordingly, some of the policy issue amendments that were accepted by the government are Hydro-power Development policy 1992, Water Resources Act 1992, Electricity Act 1992, Electricity Rules 1993 and Electricity tariff Rules 1993.

These legal amendments include, among other things, establishment and operations procedures of power industry, time bound and transparent facilities, subsidies and co-operation to be provided to the private sector. In 1992, an electricity development center was established with a view to develop hydro-power and private investment in this sector. In addition, Electricity Tariff Commission was formed in 1993 with a view to keeping the procedure of electricity tariff systematic and transparent to keep it out of government control. As a result of the legal provisions, various proposals were received by the government from foreign private sector in the development of hydro-power and as a result two projects namely Khimtikhola (60 MW) and Bhotekoshi (36 MW) were constructed with foreign private sector investment.

Petroleum Product sector

Rapid increase in the rate of urbanization (about 14 per cent of people reside in urban areas), expansion in road facilities, increasing number of vehicles (both public and private), modernization of agriculture (use of tractors in ploughing and use of pump set in irrigation), expansion in the industrial sector have brought among other things increasing trend of petroleum products in Nepal. The increasing demand for petroleum product is solely met by imports because Nepal has no proven deposits of petroleum product.

Nepal Oil Corporation is the sole distributor of petroleum products in the country. The Corporation is responsible for import, store and distributing petroleum products throughout the country. The Corporation has imported petroleum products in order to meet the domestic demand. The petroleum product consumption has an increasing trend. The annual growth rate of petroleum was 10.7 per cent during 1994/95–1998/99 (Table 2). This reveals that the annual increase in demand for petroleum product is 10.7 per cent. The total value of the petroleum product during the same period, on an average was 33 per cent of merchandise export. It indicates that Nepal has to spend 33 per cent of total export earnings to import petroleum products only. The expenditure on the petroleum product is increasing. The annual growth rate of expenditure was 20.1 per cent during the same period. This high growth rate of expenditure on petroleum products will have adverse effect on the balance of payment situation of the country.

TABLE 1.24
Consumption of Petroleum products and Its Related Expenditure

Year	*Consumption of Petroleum products (in KL)*	*Expenditure (in million Rs.)*	*POL Products Import as per cent of Merchandise Export*
1994–95	516331	5346040	30.3
1995–96	582260	6324.70	31.8
1996–97	633516	7448.70	32.9
1997–98	709724	10324.10	37.6
1998–99	775869	11136.10	31.2
Growth Rate	10.7	20.1	-

Source: Economic Survey, 2001.

Concluding Remarks

Woody and non-woody biomass fuels (including agricultural waste and animal dung) currently meet 90 per cent of Nepal's energy requirements. Rural population in Nepal depends mainly on woodfuel gathered from surrounding environment. However, in urban and semi-urban areas of Nepal woodfuel became a monetized commodity, distributed through commercial marketing networks. In contrast, the rural people use woodfuel to meet their primary energy requirement at free of cost. Rural people usually gather fuel-wood in winter season either from community forest or from their own farmland forest. In Nepal the rate of deforestation exceeds the rate of reforestation. It means the country may be converted into desert in the near future. So, there is an urgent need to conserve remaining forest of the country.

The broad conservation measures of existing forest are possible only when the alternative energy development program in the rural areas of the country is launched. Nepal has great prospects to develop and generate small hydropower in rural area where supply can be facilitated at the minimum cost. As stated above Nepal has large untapped water resources. However its use needs a huge investment that Nepal alone cannot afford. So, the mobilization of bilateral as well as multilateral resources is a must.

Annexure

TABLE I
Energy Consumption

	Energy Consumption					
Years	*Fuelwood (MT.)*	*Ag.Res. (MT.)*	*Anm.Waste (MT.)*	*Coal (MT.)*	*Petroleum (KL.)*	*Elect. (MWh)*
1984/85	9,465	2,105	1,850	145	147	287
1985/86	9,669	2,137	1,878	17	139	320
1986/87	9,769	2,281	1,898	91	177	382
1987/88	9,953	2,414	1,981	84	171	449
1988/89	10,142	2,554	1,938	76	185	479
1989/90	10,256	2,707	1,959	12	223	525
1990/91	10,503	2,864	1,979	81	230	589
1991/92	10,780	3,031	2,000	92	293	652
1992/93	10,979	3,207	2,021	110	359	694
1993/94	11,460	3,288	2,094	104	353	706
1994/95	11,715	3,418	2,124	113	382	787
Growth rate	2.0%	4.5%	1.3%	-2.2%	9.1%	9.6%

Source: WECS, 1996.

TABLE II
Consumption of Energy (in '000GJ)

Years	*Fuel. wood*	*Ag. waste*	*Ani. waste*	*Total*	*Coal*	*POL*	*Elect*	*Total*	*G.Total*
1984/85	158539	26439	20146	205124	3642	6725	1033	11400	216524
1985/86	161956	26841	20451	209248	427	6359	1152	7938	217186
1986/87	163631	28649	20669	212949	2286	8098	1375	11759	224708
1987/88	166713	30320	20887	217920	2110	7823	1616	11549	229469
1988/89	169879	32078	21105	223062	1909	8464	1724	12097	235159
1989/90	171788	34000	21334	227122	301	10202	1890	12393	239515
1990/91	175925	35972	21551	233448	2035	10523	2120	14678	248126
1991/92	180565	38069	21780	240414	2311	13405	2347	18063	258477
1992/93	183898	40280	22009	246187	2763	16424	2498	21685	267872
1993/94	191955	41297	22804	256056	2612	16150	2541	21303	277359
1994/95	196226	42930	23130	262286	2839	17477	2833	23149	285435

Source: Calculated from Annex II

TABLE III
Population, GDP and Energy

Year	*Population**	*GDP***	*NGDP***	*Commercial***	*POL Prod***	*Electricity***
1991	18.49	59768	31396	12.49	10.31	1.87
1992	18.94	62537	34461	14.70	10.57	2.13
1993	19.34	64586	36690	21.01	16.37	2.34
1994	19.86	69686	39669	21.10	15.49	2.39
1995	20.34	71685	41768	21.78	16.62	2.56
1996	20.83	75773	44534	23.40	17.73	2.81
1997	21.33	79388	46859	28.90	22.72	3.07
1998	21.84	82116	49249	33.70	23.61	3.28
1999	22.36	85789	52028	38.00	27.06	3.54
2000	22.9	91317	55878	42.75	30.22	3.79
2001	23.45	96612	59759	46.33	32.22	4.60

Source: ** Economic Survey, MOF/HMG, 2001
* Statistical Pocket Book, 2000.

Note:
pop = population in million
GDP = Gross Domestic Product in million rupees,
NGDP = non-agricultural GDP in million rupees.
Com. = commercial energy (in million GJ),
POL = petroleum product consumption (in million GJ),
Elect = electricity consumption(in millionGJ), and

TABLE IV
Population, GDP and Energy Consumption

Year	*Poplation in million*	*GDP in million Rs.*	*Agri. GDP in million Rs.*	*Nagri. GDP in million Rs.*	*Petro-leum in '000toe*	*Elect. in '000toe*	*Total comm. energy in '000toe*	*Total energy cons. in '000toe*
1	2	3	4	5	6	7	8	9
1985	15.9	44441	22761	21680	151	51	255	5035
1986	16.3	46512	23376	23136	158	24	267	5149
1987	16.8	47427	23213	24214	164	27	201	5189
1988	17.2	50761	24735	26026	193	32	279	5377
1989	17.6	53518	26260	27258	186	38	274	5482
1990	18.1	56151	27774	28377	204	40	289	5610
1991	18.49	59768	28372	31396	242	44	293	5688

1	2	3	4	5	6	7	8	9
1992	18.94	62531	28070	34461	248	50	346	5901
1993	19.39	64586	27896	36690	384	55	493	6168
1994	19.86	69686	30017	39669	374	56	495	6294
1995	20.34	71685	29917	41768	390	60	511	6436
1996	20.83	75773	31239	44534	416	66	549	6604
1997	21.33	79388	32529	46859	533	72	677	6862
1998	21.84	82116	32867	49249	554	77	791	7112
1999	22.36	85789	33761	52028	635	83	892	7350

Source: Economic Survey, MOF/HMG, 2001.

Statistical Pocket Book, CBS/HMG, 2000.

TABLE V
Basic Energy Conversions

Unit	*Gigajoules (GJ)*	*Tonnes of coal equivalent*	*Tonnes of oil equivalent*
Tonnes of coal equivalent	29.307600	1.000000	0.680272
Tonnes of oil equivalent	43.082200	1.470000	1.000000

TABLE VI
Energy Content of Traditional Fuels

Fuel	*Physical Unit*	*GJ*	*tce*	*toe*	*Others*
Fuel wood	Ton	16.7	0.57	0.39	1.43 m^3
	Cu.m.	11.7	0.4	0.27	700kg
Charcoal	Ton	28.9	0.99	0.67	2.86 m^3
	Cu.m.	10.1	0.35	0.23	350kg
Animal dung	Ton	10.9	0.37	0.25	–
Biogas	000 cu.m.	24.2	0.83	0.56	–
Agric. Waste	Ton	12.6	0.43	0.29	–

TABLE VII
Energy Content of Commercial Fuels

Fuel	*Natural Unit*	*Gj*	*Tce*	*toe*	*Others*
Diesel	K litre	37.8	1.29	0.88	0.826 ton
	Ton	46.0	1.57	1.07	12101
LDO	K litre	39.3	1.34	0.91	0.853 ton
	Ton	46.0	1.57	1.07	11721
Petrol	K litre	33.4	1.14	0.78	0.709 ton
	Ton	47.2	1.61	1.10	14111
Kerosene	K litre	36.3	1.24	0.84	0.778 ton
	Ton	46.6	1.59	1.08	12851
Av.Tur.	K litre	36.3	1.23	0.84	0.776 ton
	Ton	46.6	1.59	1.08	12881
F. Oil	K litre	41.3	1.41	0.96	0.934 ton
	Ton	44.3	1.51	1.03	10711
LPG	Ton	49.2	1.68	1.14	-
Coal	Ton	25.2	0.86	0.59	-
Electricity	MWh	3.6	0.12286	-	-
	Ton	46.6	1.57	1.07	1210
Natural Gas	1000 m^3	36	1.56	1.09	-

Source: ADB, 1992, WECS 1994, PEP 1995.

TABLE VIII
Structure of Fuel Consumption

Standard Weightage

Year	*Fuel wood*	*Agri-culture Waste*	*Animal Dung*	*Total Tradi-tional Sources*	*Petro-leum Pro-ducts*	*Coal*	*Electri-city*	*Total comme-rcial Sources*	*Grand Total*
1	2	3	4	5	6	7	8	9	10
1980/81	3382	584	445	4411	117	49	14	180	4591
1981/82	3491	593	452	4536	113	37	16	166	4702
1982/83	3572	602	459	4633	133	42	20	195	4828
1983/84	3645	611	466	4722	151	83	21	255	4977
1984/85	3720	620	473	4813	158	85	24	267	5080
1985/86	3800	630	480	4910	164	10	27	201	5111

1	2	3	4	5	6	7	8	9	10
1986/87	3839	672	485	4996	193	54	32	279	5275
1987/88	3912	711	490	5113	186	50	38	274	5387
1988/89	3986	753	495	5234	204	45	40	289	5523
1989/90	4031	798	500	5329	242	7	44	293	5622
1990/91	4128	844	506	5478	248	48	70	346	5824
1991/92	4236	893	511	5640	384	54	55	493	6133
1992/93	4315	945	516	5776	458	65	57	580	6356
1993/94	4504	969	535	6008	389	61	59	509	6517
1994/95	4604	1007	543	6154	414	67	66	547	6701
1995/96	4707	1047	550	6304	421	72	66	559	6863

Source: Economic Survey 1996, HMG.

CHAPTER TWO

Poverty and Human Resource Development

2.1 HUMAN RESOURCE DEVELOPMENT IN NEPAL: ADVANCEMENT AND DISTRESS*

Human resource development (HRD) is defined as the process of improving the quality and efficiency of the people or labour force. The quality and efficiency can be achieved through education, training, manpower planning and management. Advancement in human lives may create healthy society that can contribute to the developmen process of a nation. Low level of human development causes lower level of economic growth and the lives of the poor wil further deteriorate which leads to malnourishment, poo health, poor education etc. Nepal has already implemente eight Five Year plans whose main thrust was on economi growth. It is now evident that income inequalities an impoverishment are damaging the social, political an economic structure of Nepal.

Nepal is primarily an agricultural country with a estimated population of 21 million of which nine-tenths resid in rural areas. Nearly half of the Gross Domestic Produ (GDP) originate from agriculture. Land distribution is ver

---

* Modified from the original paper published in VIKAS, A Journ of People Environment and Development, Vol. 17, No. 2, 199 pp. 65-70.

skewed resulting in the uneven distribution of income. The bottom 40 per cent of agricultural households occupy only 9 per cent of total agricultural land area whereas the top 6 per cent of the agricultural households occupy more than 33 per cent of total agricultural land (CBS). Nepal is one of the poorest countries in the world. The World Development Report (1997) ranked Nepal as ninth from bottom with respect to per capita GNP. Likewise, the Human Development Report (1997) placed Nepal at 154th position among the 174 countries of the world in terms of human development aspect.

Poverty Profile of Nepal

There is huge literature about poverty in Nepal. Among them are multiple Household Surveys, Poverty and Incomes Surveys conducted by Nepal Rashtriya Bank and World Bank respectively. There are other individual researchers' reports also.

According to these surveys poverty is widespread in Nepal (The World Bank's estimate shows 71 per cent while the World Development Report (1997) estimated that 53.1 per cent of the population resides under the poverty line having income less than one dollar a day. Recently, Central Bureau of Statistics (CBS) conducted a survey in order to estimate the absolute poor in Nepal, based on the consumption parameters. The report revealed that 45 per cent of the population is under poverty line. The poverty is increasing in Nepal. The country is not able to reduce a sufficient profile of poverty, but identification is not made regarding the people who are poor and how to reach them? However, the approach paper of Ninth Plan (1997-2002) clearly sets its main objective to reduce the number of poor by generating employment and raising income of the people who are under the poverty line.

Trends in Growth Rate and Human Development

From the human development perspective, economic growth is not an end in itself. It is a means to lead human to its progress. The economic growth rate, whether it is high or not, is a matter of concern. But more attention must go to the structure and quality of the growth to ensure that it is directed towards supporting human development, reducing, poverty, protecting environment and ensuring sustainability. Mostly, the economic growth of developing countries is tended towards jobless, ruthless, voiceless, rootless, and futureless people. Nepal has an average growth rate of 2-3 per cent annually for the past decades. The growth rate of Nepal has been ineffective due to the reason that poverty in Nepal is chronic and increasing continuously. So, determined efforts are needed to avoid such directionless growth rate of the economy.

Though Nepal has resource endowment, mostly the water resources with a capacity of generating 83 thousand MW hydro-electricity, this immense resource has hardly been harnessed (less than one percent). Where can a beginning be made in Nepal to transform its economy and human development in the twenty-first century?. Obviously, there are many issues which draw attention of the policy makers. The fundamental issue, which figures in every policy agenda, is about the adequate investment in the people so that people are converted from the liability to the assets. The empowerment of the people in economic activities will be possible only if a concerted plan is formulated to:

- Provide universal primary education,
- provide basic health care for all,
- provide safe drinking water for the entire population,
- provide adequate nutrition for all malnourished children,
- provide institutional credit for small and marginal farmers,
- construct small irrigation projects,
- construct rural roads,
- create self-employment opportunities, and
- expand programmes for the control of population growth by means of family planning services.

Human Advancement and Distress

Efforts are continuing for the improvement of human resources since the country has experienced planned development. These efforts could not improve the human resources with respect to human development and poverty alleviation. The human advancement and distress are attempted to analyze from the point of view of the social and economic indicators. The adult literacy rate increased from 13 per cent to 26 per cent during 1970 to 1933. There are 74 per cent of adult population still illiterate. Public expenditure on education increased more than 7 times during the same period vis-a-vis half of the children dropped before reaching fifth grade.

From these statistics we can conclude that the distress of human resource development outweighs the progress with respect to education.

The health and economic indicators have also little impact on the human resource development of Nepal despite many efforts made since the middle of the 19th century.

Firstly, the expenditure on health as percentage of GDP (2.2 percent) in 1990 was higher than in any other SAARC country. But about four-fifth of the population is deprived of basic sanitation facilitates and more than half have no access to potable water facility.

Secondly, the food production increased by 14 per cent between 1980 and 1993, whereas two-third of all under five deaths are due to malnutrition.

Thirdly, the use of contracep-tives among married women increased dramatically by 23 times between 1970 and 1993 from a very low level of one per cent in 1970 (see, *Haq*: 1997) vis-a-vis the population growth rate rose from 2 per cent per annum in 1960 to 2.6 per cent in 1980-90.

Another social indicator shows that the infant mortality rate has declined from 190 per 1000 live births in 1960 to 79 in 1996, whereas stunting occurs in two-third of all children in Nepal. The earned income share of women in Nepal is 26 per cent which is the highest in the SAARC region whereas Nepal is only one of the two countries of the world where females live shorter than males. The adult female literacy rate is also only 13 percent, the lowest in SAARC. The per capita income has more than doubled in the last two decades but the current per capita income is the lowest in SAARC region.

Prerequisites for Human Resource Development

Regarding the HRD, let us examine the conditions currently available in Nepal. Housing units, their structure, characteristics and facilities are largely related to the living standard of the population of the country. The well-being of the people primarily depends on the quality and quantity of housing available. Occupancy of housing units by Nepalese people is satisfactory for the reason that about 94 per cent of the population have their own houses. But the quality of majority of the houses is very low. The average number of rooms per house is 3.04 and the average area of dwelling is 603.85 square feet. The presence of conveniences in household is far from satisfactory. The available conveniences are concentrated in urban areas than in rural one. About 14 per cent of households in Nepal have access to electricity for lighting. In urban areas, the proportion of household using electricity is 80 per cent whereas only 10 per cent households have access to those facilities in rural areas.

Similarly, about one per cent of households have telephone facility and on the whole 22 per cent of the households have access to the toilet facilities. Only 18 per cent of the households in the rural part of the country have access to toilets in contrast with the 65 per cent in urban areas. One of the survey has mentioned that only 52.2 per cent of housing units in rural and urban Nepal respectively were made of brick or stone joined either by mud or cement plastered or not plastered (1988). The situation has not improved during the decade. The prevailing situation of water supply is not satisfactory despite the large amount of money invested in the sector. On the whole, nearly 33 per cent of households have access to piped water but 8 per cent have private connections. About 46 per cent households depend upon wells, not acceptable from a health point of view. On the other hand 21 per cent of households depend on largely unreliable sources like river and spring water (CBS, 1996).

The literacy rate is not satisfactory in Nepal. Only 39.6 per cent (1991) of the population of six years and older are literate in Nepal who can simply read and write. The disparity in literacy rates between male and female is high. About 54.5 per cent of the males are literate as compared to 25 per cent of the females. The health services are not available adequately. Only 36 per cent children are fully immunized and disparity between males and females is 4 per cent.

Income and Consumption Disparities

The average households income in Nepal is NRs. 43,732 per annum while per capita income is NRs. 7690 (CBS, 1996). The variation in income is wide. The average per capita income is more than twice the average rural per capita income. Among urban areas, the urban Kathmandu valley stands first having far higher income than the average, i.e. more than three times the average for Nepal as a whole in per capita terms. Similarly, there is low average per capita income in western part of the country compared to eastern part. In Nepal, the bottom 80 per cent of households earn 50 per cent of total income while the top 20 per cent earn the remaining 50 per cent of income (CBS, 1996). On the basis of food, housing and non-food items, the measurement of total annual households consumption is calculated. The variation in household's consumption is closer. Similarly, the bottom 50 per cent of the households account for 26 per cent of consumption while the top 20 per cent account for 45 per cent of consumption (CBS: 1996).

Policies to Improve the Human Resource Development

Nepal should be prudent to optimize its scarce resources through proper allocation of development expenditure. Over the past four decades, Nepal has spent a large amount to improve the well-being of people. The basic services, which men need, are education, basic health care and nutrition, water supply and sanitation, and reproductive health. The growth rate of economy will not decline with human resource development. The equality in income distribution is a necessary factor for the development of human resources. The more equal the distribution of resources, the more likely that income growth will be reflected in an improvement of each individual of the society. To put this fact into practice, the expansion of economic activity in the country is needed.

The policies should be focused on the upliftment of absolute poor by providing adequate institutional credit, which created employment opportunities in the economy. Consequently income of the people will also rise. In this connection, a prudent and moral government with good governance can greatly influence the state of human development by channelizing a high proportion of public revenue into priority social sectors (basic education, basic health care, empowerment of the poor people by asset, rural roads, small irrigation projects, upliftment of backward classes and so on). Economic growth thus, is finally translated into improvement of human development through the expansion of income earning opportunities. As stated above, more than 45 per cent of the total population resides under absolute poverty. More people of this category are constrained by poor access to productive assets, particularly, land, credit and physical infrastructure. Therefore, the policies should be formulated by the state to empower the poor people with these facilities.

The Human Development Report 1996 clearly guides the policies for employment creating growth. Clear political commitment for full and faster employment led growth, sustained investments in people, increase in productivity and wages, pro-employment incentives and other access to productive assets, equal excess to social services, expanded opportunities of disadvantaged groups etc. are the actions recommended by the report for the human resource development. The specific policies for the development of human resource and poverty reduction are: land reforms, credit reforms, mobilizing saving and investment, co-operation between the public and private sectors etc. Although Nepal already had a long history of experimentation with land reforms, the successful implementation has not yet taken place. Meaningful land reforms in Nepal may be difficult to implement in the current structure of power. However, even without land reforms many steps can be taken to review the agricultural sector. As mentioned above the rural people can benefit from the provision of agricultural infrastructure such as irrigation, which reaches small farmers, generous credit subsidies, agricultural extension service, access to new technologies, farm to market roads, and incentives of international prices.

Conclusion

Nepal is one of the poorest countries of the World. About 50 per cent of its population is under absolute poverty. Agriculture is the main source of livelihood of the people. Only 39.6 per cent of the population, six years and older, are literate in Nepal who can simply read and write. Nepal has average economic growth rate of 2–3 per cent annually for the past few decades. It shows that the progress in economy is far from expectation. Majority of the people are deprived of basic human needs such as food, clothing and shelter. In such a situation, other facilities such as education, health, adequate nutrition, drinking water, institutional credit etc. are beyond the expectation of the majority of the people in Nepal. The human distress in Nepalese context outweighs the human progress with respect to education, health, nutrition, life expectancy, drinking water facility, mortality, and gender equality. A few percentage of the population have access to other facilities such as electricity, telephone, latrines, and drinking water, while a large percentage of the population remains on dark side. These available facilities are concentrated in urban areas of the country whereas 90 per cent of the population resides in rural area. The variation in income distribution in Nepal is wider. The top 20 per cent earn the 50 per cent of income in Nepal.

The government has to play a vital role in extending social services although the large void could be fulfilled by the civil society itself. But now-a-days private initiatives are getting organized all over Nepal with or without government help. The government often pre-empted the legitimate role of the private sector and could not provide the investment it was supposed to make. This is also the cause of poorly paid civil servants, which are tempted for corruption. The decision makers strangulate the economy and enrich themselves rather than the nation. So, there is no strong desire and commitment on the part of the government to cope with the problem of human resource development. Whatever policies are designed to cope with the problems of human resource development, they are delinked with the implementation. These contrast complexities of policy designing and implementation should be joined together to optimize the use of scarce resources for the optimum benefits of the people who are deprived severely.

2.2 POVERTY IN NEPAL: SOME THEORETICAL CONSIDERATIONS AND POLICY ISSUES*

Poverty is defined as the state of the society or a mass of people or a family or an individual, whose consumption standard fall short of the norms or whose income lie below that line (*Jain*; 1981). The people are said to be absolute poor, whose level of income in unable to meet the minimum human basic needs. Instead, the human development report however added human dimensions such as education, health etc. Different scholars working in different areas have adopted different basis and processes to define the poverty line. Among the indices used in estimating the incidence of poverty is the head count ratio, denoted by H or P_0.

H or P_0 is defined as,

H or $P_0 = q/n$

* Modified from the original paper published in Tribhuvan University Journal, Vol. XX, No. 1, 1997, pp. 119-36

where,

q = the number of poor who are ranked according to income, and

n= total number of people in the universe.

Head count ratio measure is although simple to interpret and calculate, but it is sensitive to the extent of inequality among the poor and does not consider the depth of poverty or the degree of shortfall in income. Another measure of poverty index was developed, popularly known as poverty gap ratio, first used by United States Social Security Administration to measure the aggregate shortfall of income from this poverty line. It is a Gini ratio of the income distribution of households falling below the poverty line. The poverty gap ratio has four step procedure in order to find out the depth of the poverty.:

- Subtract the income level of each unit from the poverty line income,
- Divide the difference by the poverty line income,
- Obtain the ratio of overall poor in the population, and
- Divide the total by the population size.

The poverty gap ratio (P^1) based on the above procedure is defined as

$$P = 1/N\sum_{\theta}^{np} \quad (yp\text{-}yi/yp)$$

where,

yp = Poverty line income

yi = Individual income

N = Total population

NP = No. of people below the poverty line.

Poverty gap ratio ignores vital information which can be derived from the need count ratio (P_0) which provides the number of people below the poverty line. These two indices discussed above, of the measurement of poverty, are incomplete. They do not measure the poverty in depth separately. So, Prof. Amartya Sen combined the above two indices and developed his own third index with necessary modifications for large and small poverty (Sen; 1987). Amartya Sen's index is basically based on the head count index P_0, poverty gap ratio p_1 and the Gini coefficient of the poor.

Sen's index = $P_1 [1-G] + P_0 G$

where

P_0 and P_1 are defined above and G is the Gini coefficient.

The appropriate and widely used method of income is the Gini coefficient. The method of Gini coefficient is derived from the Lorenz curve. It is defined as the area between the Lorenz curve and the line of perfect quality, divided by the area of the triangle under (above) the diagonal. When there is perfect equality in the data set, the Lorenz curve will overlap with the perfect quality line implying the value of the Gini coefficient. Gini coefficient will be equal to zero. On the other hand, if there is perfect inequality in the data set, then the value of Gini coefficient will be equal to one. These are therefore, the extreme values of Gini coefficient. Thus,

$$O \leq G < 1$$

Practically, Gini coefficient can be calculated by using the following formula for individual and group data:

For individual data

$$G.C. = \frac{1}{2n^2\mu} \sum_{I=1}^{n} \sum_{j=1}^{n} (y_i - y_j)$$

$$= 1 + \frac{1}{n} - 2/n^2\mu(y_1 + 2y_2 + .. + = ny_{n)}$$

where, n = number of observation,

μ = mean value of y

and for ($y_1 \geq y_2 \geq \ldots\ldots\ldots y_n$)

From the group data:

$$G = \Sigma x_i y_{i+1} - \Sigma x_{i+1} y_i$$

where, x_i = the cumulative proportion of *x* variable in the ith class interval, and

y_i = the cumulative proportion of *y* variable in the ith class interval.

If x_i and y_i are considered as two columns the above equation can be rewritten as the sum of all the (n-1) determinate values of x_i and y_i taken in two consecutive class intervals at a time. Thus,

$$\begin{bmatrix} x_i & y_i \\ x_{i+1} & y_{i+1} \end{bmatrix} \text{ for I = 1,2,3......, (n-1).}$$

As defined above the variables *x* and *y* should be measured in proportion not in the percentages. However, if these variables are calculated as percentages, each of them have to be divided by 100. In this case the Gini coefficient will be calculated as,

$$G= 1/100\ [\Sigma\, x_i y_{i+1} - \Sigma\, x_{i+1}\, y_i] \text{ per cent.}$$

$$G= 1/(100)^2\ [\Sigma\, x_i y_{i+1} - \Sigma\, x_{i+1}\, y_i]$$

In other words, if G is equal to zero, there is perfect equality in the distribution of income to the population under consideration and if G is equal to one, there is perfect inequality of income to the population under consideration.

Therefore, it can be concluded that the higher will be the inequality of the variables under consideration and vice versa. The following procedure should be applied when calculating the Gini coefficient:

1. Arrange the data either in ascending or descending order.
2. Obtain the cumulative frequencies.
3. Express the data in percentage stated in procedure (2).
4. Take the data of procedure (3) and express them in the form to determinate and obtain the overall sum.

Another measure of the poverty index used by the Human Development Report 1996 has the following formulation. Before describing the poverty index, it is necessary to make brief discussion about the human development index of the HDR (1966) is primarily based on the three indicators:

1. Life expectancy at birth,
2. Educational attainment, and
3. The standard of living as measured by real GDP per capita.

For any components of the HDR individual indices were computed according to the general formula by the HDR is given by

$$\text{HDI} = \frac{\text{Active } x \text{ value} - \text{minimum } xi \text{ value}}{\text{Maximum } xi \text{ value} - \text{Minimum } xi \text{ value}}$$

the minimum and maximum value of *xi* can be determined by standard norms.

The construction of income index is rather complicated and different. Suppose *y* is the highest income and y^* is the mean income of the population under consideration and any income about y^* is discounted using the following formulation based on Atkinson's formula for the utility of income:

Thus,

$$W(y) = y^o \text{ for } O>y>y$$
$$= y^o + 2\,[\,(y - y^o)\,1/2]\text{ fj or } y^o < y < y^o$$
$$= y^o + 2\,(y^o - ½) + 3\,[(y - 2y^o)\,1/3\,] \text{ for } 2y^o < y < 3y^o$$

and so on

A Brief Review Of Standard Of Living Survey (National Planning Commission)

Recently a living standard survey, report has been published by the NPC/HMG with a view to provide information and database for the living standards of people of Nepal. The survey report is fully devoted to measure the living standards of people through consumption. In nominal terms the bottom 50 per cent of households account for 26 per cent consumption while the top 20 per cent account for 45 per cent of consumption. (CBS; 1996). Similarly, it provides the average households income for the whole of Nepal is N Rs. 43732 per annum while per capita income is N Rs. 7790 From this fact one can asses, that over 50 per cent of the population resides under below poverty line. The world development report has clearly shown the percentage of poor of the total population is 53.1 per cent. Their per capita income is less than US $ 100 per annum. (World Bank; 1994) The distribution of income in nominal terms: the bottom 80 per cent of households earns 50 per cent of total income whil the top 20 per cent of household earn the rest of 50 per cent of income (CBS; 1996).

There is extreme inequality of distribution of income regardless of consumption. Therefore, the vulnerable groups of people have no other access facilities, which could not be harnessed by their own ability. Poor people whatever their number, owned small piece of land and poor housing and sanitation condition mostly in rural areas of the country. Dealing with this reason the concentration index for the total land operated is 0.54. This reflects the presence of large number of small farms in the country. It clearly shows that the bottom 40 per cent of agricultural households operated only 9 per cent of total agricultural land area, while the top 6 per cent of agricultural households on the other hand occupied more than 33 per cent of total land. This reflects the presence of the farm size distribution is small. As a consequence, there are 40 per cent small farmers who owned less than 0.5 ha. of land while there are 13 per cent large farmers who occupied 2 ha. and over. The above three indicators revealed that more improvements would be made from both the public as well as private sector in order to maintain the distribution of income and the assets regardless of health, education, drinking water, sanitation, family planning etc. to alleviate the poverty.

This NLSS has estimated the poverty rates for Nepal. Poverty rates have been calculated on the basis of Head count Index. This measure represents the percentage of population, which had an annual per capita consumption level below the poverty line i.e. incidence of poverty. This survey has set the cut off land of consumption level at N Rs. 4404. Similarly, the survey accounts the second measure, the property gap, goes same way to address the shortcomings of the head count index. This measure reflects the distance between the consumption levels of the poor and the poverty line already mentioned above. The incidence of poverty as a whole is 42 per cent in Nepal. In urban areas the rate is 23 per cent while in rural areas it is 44 per cent. It has also removed that rural poverty is deeper and more severe than urban poverty (CBS; 1996).

The Capability Poverty Measure:

The Human Development Report HDR (1996) defines the Capability Poverty Measure (CPM) as a genius index composed of three indicators that reflects the percentage of the population with capability shortfalls in three basic dimensions of human development, living a healthy well nourished life, having the capability of safe and healthy reproduction and being literate and knowledgeable. The three corresponding indicators are the percentage of children under five who are underweight. The percentage of births unattended by trained health personnel and the percentage of women aged 15 years and above who are illiterate. The aggregation of the poverty index can be obtained by taking the average of the three chosen variables under consideration. Let X_1 be the proportion of births unattended by trained health personnel, X_2 be the proportion of underweight children under age five and X_3 be the proportion of female illiteracy rate.

Then we have the CPM index as:

$$\text{CPM index} = \frac{X_1 + X_2 + X_3}{3}$$

$$\text{In general, CPM} = \frac{X_1 + X_2 + X_n}{n} = \frac{\Sigma X_i}{x}$$

Socio-Economic Structure of Nepal

Nepal as a poor country, some areas or enclosures of glittering modernity and its higher income groups live at levels of affluence, greatly exceeding the average affluence of the people of richer countries (*Giller*, 1982). Nepal is a tiny state and India-locked rather than landlocked and politically insatiable after the restoration of multi-party system in 1990. There is a vast gap of standard of living of the people in Nepal where the top 10 per cent have the new fate to become affluent from the dubious means whereas above 60 per cent remains under the misty condition who are accountable for absolute poor (World Bank; 1990). The good society is not identified with the affluent society or a better society with a more affluent one. A wide gap of income and wealth, power and apparatus plate from the mass of population in Nepal reduce the middle class in numbers (NPC; 1992). By virtue of the popular mass movement in Nepal of 1990. Most of the middle class people have new fate to become affluent leaving the majority of people in poverty and deprivation. The political leaders of Nepal, more or less, are turned into the growth of new-catalysts of that they are less responsive to the needs of the masses. The practice of corruption and immoral behaviour of Nepalese government led the development work under dilemma so that there is low level of income of people, which resulted from the wide-spread unemployment and stagnant economic growth or even further deterioration.

The powerful elite's who govern the country are greatly influenced either by the foreigners or by the nation's capitalists. As a result of the concert of the powerful, the voices of the masses of people remain muted (*Dhungel*; 1992,1995).

Diversification of Resources into Unproductive Sectors:

The rich in Nepal are not noted for their frugality or for their design to save and invest substantial proportion of their income in the economy. Experience shows that landlords; businessmen, politicians and other rich elites are known to allocate much of their income on imported luxury goods, expensive houses, foreign travel and investment in other expensive and scarce goods and banking accounts. Such savings and investment do not add to the nation's productive resources. They, in fact, represent substantial drains on these resources. That the income derivation is often extracted from the sweat and toll of common uneducated and unskilled labour. Unfortunately, the majority of people in Nepal are under below poverty line, whereas the politicians and other elite classes have the new fate to become affluent. (*Dhungel*; 1996).

Incidence of Poverty in Nepal

Various efforts were made from the long back in Nepal to identify and alleviate poverty. As its consequences, we have at least the poverty profile judged from the different criteria. The survey on employment, income distribution and consumption patterns, as the first of this kind was conducted by the National Planning Commission in Fiscal Year (FY) 1976-77 to define and quantify the level of poverty in Nepal. This survey had fixed the criteria for the delineation of the poverty line, it was the subsistence level of income and expenditure. The income level of Rs. 2 per capita per day at 1976-77 prices was taken as the minimum subsistence level of income. Similarly, the World Bank study group have suggested an income of US$ 40 per person per year at 1976-77 prices as the poverty line for Nepal. This was however, adjusted to US$ 150 per capita per year at 1988/89 prices. The third possible definition is one suggested by Lipton. He has defined the poor as those whose food expenditure absorb 70 per cent or more of the total expenditure (*Lipton;* 1983). Based on these three basic definitions the incidence of poverty in Nepal is given in the following table:

TABLE 2.1
Incidence of Poverty Based on Different Criteria

Line	*Rural*	*Urban*	*Total*	*Rural*	*Urban*	*Total*	*Rural*	*Urban*	*Total*
NPC	29	17	28	55	19	52	42	15	40
US$ 150	69	51	68	78	32	75	74	42	71
Lipton	70	50	68	65	52	64	68	51	66

Note: Figures are expressed in percentages.
Source: World Bank, Nepal Poverty and Incomes.

There is no identical result about the number of absolute poor in Nepal. Different studies conducted by different institutions have the different results. However, the poverty in absolute terms is over 60 per cent of the total population while the eighth five-year plan (1992-1997) has estimated the ratio at 49 per cent.

A new concept is developed by the human development report (1996). Accordingly, it has listed 101 countries as poor according to the criteria of the Capability Poverty Measure (CPM). According to this criteria, Nepal is listed last. Followings are the basic indicators of Nepal, which are taken from the HDR (1996):

1. Births unattended by the trained health personal 1983-94 in per cents are 94.
2. Underweight children under age five in per cent 1985-95 is 51, and
3. Female illiteracy rate in per cent in 1993 is 87.

The average of these three indicators is known as the CPM index value. For Nepal, the CPM index would be 77.3 per cent. Thus, from this CPM index it is obvious that about 77 per cent of the people are incapability poor, on average in all three dimensions. For companions, the CPM indices of the SAARC countries are given in the following table:

TABLE 2.2
CPM values of SAARC Countries

(in per cent)

Country	*CPM Value*	*Rank of SAARC Countries of 101 Countries*
Sri Lanka	19.3	26
Maldives	35.5	53
Pakistan	60.8	87
India	61.5	89
Bhutan	68.2	96
Bangladesh	76.9	100
Nepal	77.3	101

Source: Human Development Report, 1996.

From the point of view of CPM value, Nepal is not only ranked last out of the 101 countries of the world but also it ranked last in its affiliated regional countries of SAARC. It means we have the poor human resource development inspite of the heavy efforts made since the last four decades.

A review of the measures was taken by the Government

to alleviate the poverty in Nepal. Steps were taken from long back to alleviate the poverty of Nepal. In FY 1975/76 the government had introduced institutional credit program through Agriculture Development Bank to the poor in-group basis. The program is termed as the Small Farmers Development Program (SFDP) which mainly provides loan to small farmers in-group basis. The criteria for identification of small farmers was fixed as a person or a family who owned 2.6 ha. of land in Tarai and one ha. of land in hills and mountains were not considered and they are illegible to form a group in order to get the institutional loan. Due to lack of proper statistics of land holding by a person or a family the identification of poor is rather a difficult task. So, the definition was modified later to consider increase as opposed to land. Families having Rs. 720 per capita or less annual income at 1978 prices were considered small farmers.

Poverty Alleviation in Seventh Plan

The Seventh Plan (1985-90) of Nepal had comprehensively set its various objectives among which the fulfillment of basic needs of the people was primarily directed towards the alleviation of poverty. This program emphasized ensuring for all people the basic means of well being, food, health and education. This program has three main parts:

(*a*) it emphasized the importance of increasing incomes through efficient labour intensive production,
(*b*) it assigned a key role in reducing poverty to public services—mass education, safe drinking water, family planning and health services, and
(*c*) it states to shift people's attention to participation.

But the top down state action backed this program and it did not improve the poor economically (*Seventh Plan* (1985-1990), *Singer,* 1988).

Policies to Fix The Standard Parameters

Virtually, Nepal is a poor country with a substantial resource constraints and diverse topographical nature on the one and India locked with open border in the southern part of the country hinder the receptive programs to launch separately on the other. So, it is difficult to reduce the poor in a considerable number. Given the constraints, Nepal could do much for reducing poverty with the proper identification of poor. Weak implementation and faulty methods of identifying past had not delivered the benefit to the target group effectively from the rural development programs. In the past no uniform parameters were used to identify the extent of poor. Poverty is a widespread phenomenon in Nepal although it has not the dependable data as regard to the magnitude of poverty in the backward and remote areas. Not a single parameter basically used is sufficient to identify the poor but various parameters should be put in practice. So, overall with a separate judgement should be implemented jointly in order to identify the poor in Nepal. Among others, the following parameters should be enforced to identify the poor in Nepalese perspective:

- Consider the size of land holding criteria.
- Consider the income and expenditure (take separately) families per capita per year.
- Consider the expenditure on education and health annually.
- Inspect the housing condition of people.

Consider the minimum income level in order to meet the basic needs of people in the growing inflationary pressure and demarked this level of income as the poverty line income. Consider the people whose income is greater than the poverty line income, as a relative poor. On the contrary, consider the people who are absolute poor to that level of income, which falls below the poverty line. The above stated criteria should be consolidated in connection with the poverty line income in order to identify the poor.

Policies to Alleviate Poverty

The low incomes and low levels of living for the poor which are manifested in poor health, nutrition and education can lower their economic productivity and thereby lead directly and indirectly to a slower growing economy. Strategies to raise the incomes and living standard of the poor contribute not only to their material well-being but also to the productivity and the income of the economy as a whole. With a substantial resource constraint and disadvantageous locations, as stated above, Nepal can implement the policies independently to reduce the poverty.

Infrastructure Development Programs

Poverty is widespread in backward rural areas of Nepal. The small-scale infrastructure development program—such as rural road construction, development of the small irrigation projects will generate additional income of the targeted population, if such public supported development works are to be performed by labour intensive techniques. The poor in rural areas will directly benefit from the public supported construction works. It will help to increase the efficiency (living condition) of the poor by increasing the volume of agricultural production in the rural areas. Therefore, it is necessary to formulate a national policy of diverting funds to such areas. People, if they are properly identified as poor before implementing such programs in the rural areas, otherwise different services and materials provided by the government as grants and subsidized rates will be utilized by relatively well off ones or by the comparatively abettor off group among the poor. The above said labour intensive public supported construction works will generate additional income and employment for the poor.

Policy of Food Security

Nepal had ample food, yet half of the population i.e. 10 millions of poor people do not share this abundance. They suffer from lack of food security caused mainly by lack of purchasing power. The term food security is devised as access by all people at all times to enough food for an active healthy life. Thus, when designing and implementing the programme of reducing poverty, it is necessary to introduce food for work in order to deliver food for all the poor people. This will increase the efficiency of poor people to take part in the public support construction work, which is basically designing to raise the income and employment to the poor.

Credit Policy

The small or poor farmers in rural areas suffer from lack of adequate capital for investing in the production-oriented sector such as in agriculture and small-scale industries. The Small Farmers Development Program (SFDP) launched through Agricultural Development Bank of Nepal has adapted production credit for rural women (PCRW) under the ministry of Local Development and the Intensive Banking Program (IBP). These programs had positive impact on the distribution of credit to the poor farmers, which has promising features such as group process and participation to promote self-help. Therefore, the government has to take effective measures of providing loans to the poor through these programs, particularly in raising the community development, income generation and additional employment. This process facilitates the channelling of other services such as literacy, training, primary health care and water supply to the poor, encourages group savings and becomes a focal point for undertaking group initiatives. Following steps are to be taken to make poverty alleviation programs effective:

- Conduct a survey to identify small farmers,
- Strengthen and manage the training for group organizers,
- Motivate the poor people for the formation of groups,
- Discourage the people who are relatively better off on their well being to take part in such a program, and
- Conduct a program to increase the efficiency of administrative staff with a highly paid remuneration and penalty provisions for effective implementation.

Education Policy

The education system should be made compulsory at the primary level by providing easy access to get the education facility. Among others, the following policies should be made effective in order to facilitate the target group:

- Conduct wide and massive literacy programs,
- Manage to provide the training for teachers locally,
- Increase the financing for primary education,
- Make compulsory education system atleast for primary level,
- Open the primary level schools in large numbers, and
- Focus to conduct the informal education system.

Health Policy

The country is still lagging far behind then other developing countries in the status of health of the population and delivery of health care especially in the rural areas. The people can cite two reasons for not getting enough health facilities. *Firstly,* the inadequate public expenditure on health cares. *Second,* In order to develop the human resources of the country, the health policy of the government should include establishing the health posts in all the village development committees for easy access for health to the poor. Thus, it is necessary to implant the policies in participating in the not income generating activities by the poor for the development of human resources such as education, hygiene and health.

The policies towards the improvement of health of the poor include:

- Consider a mass hygiene campaign, containing hygiene education and changing hygiene behaviour with rural water supplies and sanitation facilities,
- Focus on immunization, and dehydration, micro nutrient programs,
- Increase the public expenditure on health sector,
- Increase the expenditure for the fulfillment of required health manpower,,
- Conduct well targetted food security and nutrition supply programs for women and children, particularly in poor and disadvantaged communities and areas,
- Focus on primary health care and preventive measures.

Population Policy

The growth rate of the population in Nepal (2.1 per cent p.a) is approximately equal to the growth rate of GDP. In such a perspective, the economy in the given technology, will not feed the population. Therefore, Nepal has the urgent need to control the growth of population through family planning with the following policies:

- arrange the massive awareness program nation-wide,
- increase the supply of contraceptives,
- manage to train women health worker,
- increase the program of NHC and child health care,
- train the health worker locally,
- remunerate the high wages to the health worker,
- check the migrated people from the southern open border.

Agrarian Reform Policy

Above 80 per cent of the active labour force is absorbed by agricultural sector. Due to absence of the non-farm income people are compelled to live in a state of poverty. The population pressure, pushes towards to use the marginal land under cultivation. The yield per ha. is very low which is insufficient to feed the families under consideration. The inequality in the distribution of land is above 60 per cent of the total arable land. Therefore, the government should guarantee the tenancy rights by framing and enforcing the land reform program for agrarian reforms with the following policies:

- extend the market for agricultural production in rural areas,
- distribute improved seeds and fertilizers at subsidized rates to the poor who fall under the poverty line,
- construct small scale irrigation systems suitable to the topography in the participatory approach through labour intensive technique
- make arrangements to give emphasis for the development of agriculture, horticulture, livestock etc.

suitable according to the topography of the country.

- eliminate the duel ownership of land through land reform scheme.

Employment Generation and Skill Development Polices

The challenging issue of generating employment to the growing population is crucial. Facing the challenging issues, jobs for unemployed and under-employed poor, who want to work outside the agricultural sector should be created. As stated above, the public supported labour intensive construction work will have the positive impact in providing seasonal employment to the poor.. Such construction work should be implemented through the food for work program. By increasing the volume of construction work such as construction of rural road, irrigation projects, warehouse, health post, school building especially designed for employment for the short period and it will have the long run impact to raise the standard of living of poor people.

As regards skill development the government should have to run training programs to develop the skill of the poor people. The training programs such as carpentry, tailoring, embroidery, masonry, press hand, composing, electrical and general mechanics, brick production and other similar skills should be managed throughout the country for the poor who are identified under the poverty line. Such programs will create additional income through self-help employment.

Conclusion

Instead of reduction in the number of poor, various studies including of World Bank, revealed that there is continuity in the increase of poor in Nepal. The public efforts to alleviate the poverty did not succeed since the last two decades. The programs such as basic needs fulfillment and subsequent one have not shown positive impact. The SFDP program was conducted by the government through Agricultural Development Bank of Nepal. These programs are increasingly unable to cope with the extent of needs of the poor. Thus, one should clearly forward the policy of an acute need to protect the new poor and the chronically poor by introducing social assistance programs or restructuring existing ones in a way that make them politically and administratively sustainable. For the reduction of poverty permanently, it is necessary to honour poor people by their asset that is labour. Before introducing the programs for the poor, it is necessary to compile additional information about who is the poor? and how to reach them? The credit based program for the poor will be effective to initiate them to participate in the main stream of development rather than the direct public works which contributes the smoothing of consumption in the short run only.

2.3 POLICIES TOWARDS POVERTY ALLEVIATION*

Poverty is said to exist when households lack sufficient monetary income to purchase some arbitrarily defined necessities of life. The main minimum subsistence consists of essential consumption of food, housing, clothing, medical care, etc. Nepal is one of the poorest countries, with an annual per capita income of US$ 180. For several decades efforts have been made to alleviate poverty with the introduction of Basic Needs and Small Farmers Development Programs. But experiences show that the number of absolute poor continues to increase. Therefore the 'war on poverty' must still be fought.

A number of efforts by the Government have produced some success. As a result, there is a better understanding of the characteristics of poverty – that is, a poverty profile. There is no consensus about the extent of poverty. The National Planning Commission revealed that, according to the eighth plan (1992-97), 49 per cent of the total population lives in absolute poverty, whereas the World Bank estimated 70 per cent. Over 95 per cent of these reside in rural areas.

Broadly speaking, there are two possible poverty alleviation strategies in Nepal: indirect and direct.

Indirect : The indirect approach is based on the

* Published in Everest Herald, April 13, 1996

assumption that shortcomings in land, capital, credit and employment must be filled through government intervention. Poverty can be reduced to some extend by raising the growth rate of the economy as one of the most important determinants in the eradication of poverty, but Nepal's economic growth has been par with population growth.

The population growth rate has also been increasing despite efforts to reduce it through family planning programs.

The land reforms program can also be implemented to ensure reasonable distribution of land to the poor. Ownership of land is an important determinant of poverty in rural households. Most of the land in Nepal is fragmented and scarce due to the high and increasing demographic pressures. According to the 1991 agriculture survey, 70 per cent of landowners hold only 30.5 per cent of the total land cultivated with an average size of holding of less than one hectare. With such inequality, land reform is a potentially powerful direct instrument for improving the access of the poor to land and for creating the favourable initial conditions for egalitarian growth.

Land reforms aims to a shift from larger size farming to smaller size but viable family farms. However, land reform in Nepal can show few successes in enforcing the proper land-holding ceiling to the benefit of individual farmer families. After the restoration of the multi-party system in Nepal five years ago, the first elected government formulated the Eighth five Year plan (1992-97), which explicitly calls for effective lands reform. But the NC government in its three and half years of tenure failed to effectively formulate or implement a land reform program. Although the UML government came into office in 1994 with a pledge of enforcing the land reforms in order to abolish the dual ownership of land by fixing a reasonable land ceiling based on the topographical structure of the country, it also could not bring out any concrete programs and policies in its annual budget—except for the formation of a high-level Land-Reforms Commission. The present NC-headed coalition government has also committed itself to implement the land reform program without any specific policy action. However, the government of UML did distribute land to over 60 thousands squatter families in order to abolish landlessness in Nepal.

Another measure for the alleviation of poverty is to raise employment in the agricultural as-well-as non-agricultural sectors. In Nepal, over 80 per cent of the population is engaged in agricultural sector alone; where 40 per cent of them are unemployed. Poor human resource development is another cause of poverty in Nepal. Therefore, a huge government expenditure should be directed to improve the quality as well as quantity of education and health care.

The second, direct approach, to eradicating poverty includes targeting programs for the poor such as wage employment programs and promotion of self-employment. The UML government brought in a bottoms-up approach to development in order to uplift the standard of living of the poor through its "Let us Build our Village Ourselves" together with other various programs, such as construction of rural roads, small irrigation projects, health for all in a simplified manner, lower level education development, and drinking water facilities.

But these programs, except the newly named "Power to the Village" version of "Let us Build Our Village Ourselves", disappeared alongwith the collapse of the UML's minority government in September 1995. Now there are no direct programs to alleviate poverty in Nepal except through the establishment of rural financial institutions.

2.4 MICRO-HYDRO: A SUSTAINABLE MEANS TO PROVIDE BETTER ENERGY SERVICES TO THE POOR

Looking at the development of technology, there are a number of ways in generating electric energy in small scale. The small-scale electric energy generation provides a better room for the provision of energy services to the poor people. Recent technological development provides a better consecrate to develop and install small-scale electric energy projects with the mobilization of local resources. Nepal is a country with over 4000 villages and numerous strewn small sub-villages having unused resources for the development of sustainable and renewable energy projects. The people of these villages and sub-villages use biomass energy in fulfilling their primary energy needs, which had consequent adverse effects on the health of people, environmental degradation, biodiversity loss, loss of productive labour, soil erosion, desertification etc. The people of such areas are unable even to meet the minimum human basic needs such as food, shelter, cloth, health services, education, sanitation and safe water and transportation. Among the majority of the poor in Nepal 38 per cent of the total population are under absolute poverty. It means their income level is less than one US dollar a day. In order to deliver minimum human requirements to the poor people the delivery of better energy services is essential. Hence minimum basic human requirement cannot be fulfilled without the use of energy sources. In other words, energy services are the means to deliver human basic needs to the people. Production and consumption of goods and services largely depend on the services to which the energy endows with. Rural households use biomass energy with low efficient energy services, which accounts to above 90 per cent of the national energy consumption. Rural poor households overwhelmingly meet their daily energy requirement by the traditional sources of energy (fuelwood, crop residues and animal dung).

The alternative energy technology in the world today grants a better opportunity to distribute modern form of energy to the people in the diverse and dispersed remote villages of the nations of the world. Recent technological development opens wide range of application not only in the well accessed and developed area but also in the remote and under-developed areas. Similarly, it does not only concentrate on one type of energy related projects but also it has the wide range of implementation suitable to the use of local resources. Considering the electric energy projects, which can be generated using local level easily available resources such as gas, fuel cell, biomass, wind, photovoltaic, solar and micro-hydro.

Since the last four decades, efforts were made to develop various electric energy projects with a view to ease better energy services to the people and conserve the natural resources, particularly forest to safeguard and achieve the utmost economic goal of poverty alleviation and sustainable development. However, attention was focused to the use of large hydro-electric projects, which may not be applicable to distribute electric energy to the people of diverse and dispersed remote villages of the nation. Micro-hydro has immense potentiality in the context of Nepal, and existed for centuries in the form of milling. The history of modern micro-hydro power plant in Nepal is not old. The first micro-hydro power plant was installed only four decades ago. Micro-hydro electrification has marked in the five-year plans of Nepal since 1980. Policy issues on the development of micro-hydro to provide better energy services to the people of sparse villages of the country has featured in the Eighth Plan (1992) and Ninth Plan (1997). Targets for micro-hydro were set at 5 MW for each period.

With the outset of eighth plan, liberalization policy was envisaged in the overall functioning of Nepalese economy. Since then it has witnessed deregulation among other things, of the development of this sector with the abolishment of licensing requirements for micro-hydro plants as a major feature. In addition, subsidy in various forms has been a key policy feature since 1985. In the initial phase of the policy, the subsidy for new micro-hydro installation was channelled through Agriculture Development Bank of Nepal (ADB/N) with subsidy for electrical components only being provided at 75 per cent of cost for remote areas and 50 per cent for non-remote areas. However, the channel of granting subsidy is being shifted to the Alternative Energy Promotion Centre (AEPC), which was established in 1997 under the public ownership with a view to promote renewable energy technology including micro-hydro, has made some changes of the subsidy policy to the establishment of new micro-hydro projects. AEPC has created Interim Rural Energy Fund (IREF) with a view to raise the fund for granting the financial support to the new renewable energy projects, which was supported by DANIDA Energy Sector Assistance Programme (ESAP). AEPC has set the subsidy rate ranging from Rs. 8 to Rs. 70,000 depending on the KW of electricity to be generated from the new micro-hydro projects.

The development and installation of micro-hydro seems encouraging. Private investors show their interest in the establishment of such projects. As a result of the subsidy policy of the government a total of 1956 micro-hydro schemes were installed with electricity generating capacity of 13064 kW since the last four decades. Efforts were made to install micro-hydro schemes since 1962 and the pace of development has taken momentum only after the 80s. Comparing the micro-hydro distribution according to the development regions, Eastern Development Region weighs highest number of installations 665 with the electric power generating capacity of 2798 kW followed by Western Development Region 594 with the electric power generating capacity of 5328 kW, Central Development Region 397 with the electric power generating capacity of 2798 kW, Mid-western Development Region 259 with the electric power generating capacity of 1950 kW and Far Western Development Region 81 with the electric power generating capacity of 887 kW respectively.

The people of rural areas have used fuelwood for cooking and heating and kerosene for lighting in a large and uncontrollable scale. It creates an expensive social cost including health cost, labour cost in collecting firewood, indoor pollution health cost, environmental degradation, biodiversity loss and the loss of soil fertility etc. Poor people even used poor quality fuel such as crop residues and animal waste in order to meet their primary energy needs like cooking and heating. In such a given scenario of the use of energy in the rural areas, it is necessary to develop alternative source of energy that can be able to offer modern form of energy services to the poor people of rural areas. Therefore, planners and policy makers should give due attention to exploit the huge potentiality of the installation of micro-hydro schemes in the scattered and isolated villages of the country in order to provide the service of modern form of energy to the village household level. Micro-hydro schemes will provide the modern form of energy to the rural people by mobilizing local resources in a greater scale. It helps to create a just and equitable society and balance the environmental deterioration on the one hand and helps to mobilize unused resources on the local level and in turn improves the living standard of people by creating new employment opportunities on the other. Thus, the development efforts should be concentrated and diverted towards to develop and install micro-hydro to achieve twin goals of poverty alleviation and sustainable development.

2.5 ENERGY AS A CATALYST TO DISCHARGE BASIC NEEDS OF THE POOR PEOPLE

The South Asian region comprising poorest of the poor countries of the world has proportionately low level of development with respect to the consumption of commercial energy. The region is most viable and endowed with water resources to generate hydro-electricity to fulfill the gap of the shortage of power in the region. Bangladesh, India and Nepal are in need of electricity. However, individual countries like Nepal whose theoretically, high potential capacity to generate hydro-electricity (approximately 83 thousand MW among which 42 thousand MW is economically feasible), cannot itself generate it with its resources. The south Asian region, which includes Bangladesh, Bhutan, India, Maldives, Nepal, Pakistan and Sri Lanka have their common organization known as South Asia Association for Regional Cooperation (SAARC) whose aim isto prologue to develop, extend and bring regional cooperation to the common area of interest with mutual benefit. In addition the member countries of the SAARC have agreed among other things, to develop alternative energy sources to fulfill the energy requirements of the people in a sustainable manner. But the proper action has not yet been taken to develop and harness the immense potentiality of water resources of the region so far.

Nepal, a tiny country with per capita GNP amounting to US $ 220 is lowest within the countries of SAARC region and across the developing countries of the world. The population census 2001 reveals that 86 per cent of the total population resides in the rural areas of the country. Over 38 per cent of the population is under absolute poverty and mostly above 90 per cent are originated in the rural area. This situation is the outcome of the inequalities in the distribution of income and wealth. There is a wide variation between the distribution of income, consumption patterns, attitudes, aspirations and life styles of the people in Nepal. The above variables separate the elites of Nepal from the masses. Disparity in income, wealth, consumption, attitude, aspiration and lifestyle of people divide the society into various groups and as a result, the energy consumption pattern of the society also differs significantly in using the type of fuel and the level of energy consumption. Poor households use traditional sources of energy whereas wealthier households use both traditional and commercial sources of energy.

Energy is a commodity like other commodities such as food, shelter, clothing, health, education and so on. Poor people not only are characterized by the lack of adequate food, minimum required clothes, justifiable shelter, basic education and health facilities but also they are characterized by the lack of modern forms of energy. Energy is a consumer good, therefore, households demand energy to fulfill their basic energy requirement such as lighting, cooking, heating, cooling and transportation. Households consume energy because of the services of light, power and heat that it provides. Energy sources differ in their efficiency in meeting these needs—and in their capacity to do so—and also in their positive and negative side effects. The major source of energy in Nepal from the very beginning to date is fuelwood.

With increase in population, deforestation has been taking place in order to convert forest land into agricultural land. It is because increased number of people need more agricultural land for their livelihood. It brings several consequences to the availability of fuelwood. Fuelwood becomes scarce not only for the additional room for agricultural land but also for the increasing demand of fuelwood, fodder, construction materials, raw materials in the forest based industries and lack of specific policies of the government in order to conserve the forest resources. The poor people overwhelmingly reside in the rural area of the country. There is no other substitute of energy other than fuelwood, crop residues and animal waste—generally termed as traditional source of energy. As fuelwood becomes scarce, the use of crop residues and animal waste is increasing. The use of crop residues and animal dung as energy increases which creates serious effects on agricultural productivity. Animal waste serves as manure in the agricultural land. It keeps soil fertile and in turn it increases agricultural productivity. Unfortunately, people are compelled to shift its use from manure to energy.

Deforestation brings serious threat in the environmental degradation and bio-diversity loss and in turn it creates scarcity in meeting the daily energy requirement of people. The poor people who reside in the rural areas of the country use fuelwood as a major source of energy. As the process of deforestation continues at a high-speed people have to spend a lot of time and energy in collecting firewood. It poses a serious problem of the loss of their productive labour. The women and children employ their productive labour in the collection of firewood from the forest. Children of the poor households devote their time and energy in collecting firewood and fodder instead of devotion of their valuable time and energy in education. Children of such households could not attend school because they have to spend most of the time in collecting firewood and fodder.

Given the above scenarios with respect to energy consumption, a concrete policy towards the development of new and renewable sources of energy is as urgent to provide the service of modern form of energy to the poor people of the country. There has been other chatty programmes for the development of large hydro-electric projects, which are not applicable in delivering energy services to the poor in the scattered and isolated villages of the country. Although, the large hydro-electric projects have their own benefits if Nepal can launch such projects and overlook the power sharing potential for future market in the countries of SAARC region. In this respect, Nepal will become a major contributor in supplying electricity to the South Asian Region, which will earn substantial foreign exchange needed to bring sustainable development. However, lack of adequate capital is the main astounding barricade to many energy projects in Nepal. The large hydro-electric projects like Chisapani, Pancheswar and Arun III, which are in pipeline, are waiting for an appropriate investment.

On the other hand small and micro-hydro-electric projects, which have immense potentiality in Nepal can be substituted to the large hydro-electric projects. Efforts are being placed time and again to develop small and micro hydro-electric projects since the last four decades. Presently, Nepal has installed 19 big and 30 micro and small hydro-electric projects with an electricity generating capacity of 13064 and 7476 kW respectively up to the year 2001. The development of such hydro-electric projects may possibly serve the people who are under deprivation and enhance their capability to a great extent by providing modern form of energy and replace the use of traditional form of energy. The development of micro and small hydro-electric projects is suitable while considering the huge potentiality for their installation on the part of the suitable topographical structure of the country. The installation cost of such hydro-electric projects is low when compared to the cost of installing large hydro-electric projects for the reasons that mobilization of local resources is possible. Labour intensive technique could preferably be employed while installing such projects throughout the country, which promotes employment and enhances the use of local skill and increases the living standard of people by increasing the level of income.

CHAPTER THREE

Economic Modelling and Other Quantitative Approach

3.1 MACRO ECONOMIC MODELS IN DEVELOPING COUNTRIES*

Models are quantitative tools generally used by national planners to find solution for wide variety of economic planning and policy issues. In an economy where planned development exists, the input-output model is an essential tool for the determination of input to be used and output to be produced. The data required for input-output analysis is extremely a difficult task for a developing country like Nepal. Thus, the database for input-output analysis can be generated through macro-econometric modelling. Macro models are influenced by Keynesian income expenditure theory and therefore are applied to address short-term stabilization problems. There is no unanimous concensus for the models to be used in developing countries. The overall models are often conflicting because of wide range of crucial aspects of developing economies such as the nature of financial markets, the degree of capital mobility, the form and function of the exchange rate regime, the degree of wage price flexibility, expectations of forward looking and so on. (*Haque*; 1990)

The objectives of macro models for the short run and long

* *Modified from the original paper published in* Economic Review, No. 11, 1999, pp. 1-14.

run stabilization problems is to find the optimum size of investment, a tolerable rate of inflation, an acceptable ratio of deficit, an stipulated rate of growth of per capita consumption in order to increase the consumption level of poor people, a realistic level of foreign investments and to determine the optimum level of employment generation. This paper attempts to analyze the macro models for various sector on an economy on the basis of aggregate demand and supply.

Specification of the Model

To achieve the goal of macro models in developing countries, like Nepal, there is an urgent need to specify the models. Most of the developing countries are characterized by the absence of data. Therefore, the model should also be specified according to the nature and pattern of economies of the particular countries. For this reason there are substantial disagreements over the general specification of such models as well as the orders of magnitude of certain key macro economic parameters.

Aggregate Demand Model

Verbally, aggregate demand is the sum of consumption, investment, government expenditure and trade balance. Mathematically,

$$Y_t = C_t + I_t + G_t + X_t - (e^t P_t^* Z_t / P_t) + \text{error}$$

where,
t = time period,
Y_t = the real gross domestic product,
C_t = the real private consumption expenditure,
I_t = the real gross domestic investment expenditure,
G_t = the real gross government expenditure on domestic goods,
X_t = the real export,
e^t = nominal exchange rate (price of foreign currency in domestic currency terms),
Z_t = the real imports measured in terms of the foreign goods,

$P_t^* =$ foreign currency price of imports,

$P_t =$ domestic currency price of domestic output,

$e^t P_t^* / P_t =$ real exchange rate.

This aggregate demand model consists of five exogenous variables of which one is the predetermined variable i.e. government expenditure G_t. The specification of other exogenous variables including government expenditure is as follows:

Consumption Function

The consumption function is divided into two major parts. Turning to the private consumption function, thus,

$$PC_t = b_0 + b_1 r_t + b_2 Y_t^d + b_3 Pc_{t-1} + b_4 Y^d_{t-1} + \text{error}$$

where,

$b_i =$ coefficient to be determined and (i = o, 1...n)

$r_t =$ domestic rate of interest,

$Y_t^d =$ real disposable income.

The private consumption expenditure model includes the real rate of interest (r_t). This will provide the semi-elasticity of consumption measured by the parameter b_1. The other one period lag endogenous explanatory variable such as private consumption expenditure (Pc_{t-1}) provides Ratchet effect of cycle hypothesis, permanent income hypothesis and partial adjustment assumption. Similarly, the inclusion of one period lag disposable income as an endogenous explanatory variable provides a Blanchard hypothesis of finite horizons for private agents *(see, Haque: 1988)*. The consumer disposable income, the key explanatory variable in the private consumption is identified to be GDP plus the earnings on net assets held abroad minus interest paid on domestic debt and taxes.

The second macro econometric model for consumption function is the government expenditure that may be considered as the policy variables. But the developing countries governments has no discretionary power to change the government consumption expenditure in the short run. Therefore, the endogenous variable GC (government consumption) is assumed to be affected by government revenue, foreign assistance and the inclusion of lagged endogenous variable here reflects Ratchet effect.

The equation of real government consumption be

$$GC_t = \alpha_0 + \alpha_1 GR_t + \alpha_2 GC_{t-1} + \alpha_3 FA_t + e_t$$

where,

GC_t = real government consumption,
GR_t = real government revenue,
FA_t = Foreign assistance.

Investment Function

Before specifying the model for investment function, it is necessary to define what is capital stock. From the early period there are different types of interpretations for the stock of capital among economists. For some economists having interest in economic growth, capital is generally taken to mean the stock of produced means of production available to a firm or an economy at any point of time i.e., stock of fixed capital equipment. Apart from the above argument economists recently have increasingly developed special concept of capital and investment in rather different contexts. Social overhead capital refers to the road, bridges, port etc. which although not contributing directly to the production of output, but it provides the essential framework in which conventional economic activity can take place and facilitate investment. In this context, modelling in investment is rather difficult because the decision to invest in capital assets depends on expectations for the future. Haque suggested that the developing countries are characterized by the absence of data of capital stock. So, the adoption of linear formulation is to avoid the absence of capital stock data by first differentiating the equation. Thus,

$$I_t = K_0 + K_1 + r_t + K_2 Y_t + K_3 I_{t-1} + \text{error}$$

where,

I_t = investment,
r_t = real interest rate
Y_t = real output.

Now, with first differences it becomes,

$$I_t = K_1 (r_t - r_{t-1}) + K_2 (Y_t - Y_{t-1}) + K_3 I_{t-1}$$

This transformation eliminates the capital stock available for which no developing countries data are available. The private investment expenditure model would be assumed to

$$PI_t = \beta_0 + \beta_1 GDP_{t-1} + \beta_2 r_t + \beta_3 BCR_t + \text{error.}$$

where,

PI_t = private investment expenditure,
GDP_t = real gross domestic product,
r_t = real interest rate,
BCR_t = bank credit to the private sector.

The inclusion of one period lagged of real gross domestic product captured the acceleration principle. Some of various empirical studies include the GDP as an explanatory variable.

Government Investment Expenditure

Economists refer to the government investment expenditure as the policy variable. In developing countries like Nepal, the development process has been accelerated through government investment. Unlike the government consumption expenditure, the government investment expenditure is much more under government discretionary control. The government investment expenditure is assumed to effect by the government revenue and foreign assistance. Thus, one of the possible equation for public investment is

$$GI_t = l_0 + l_1 GR_t + l_2 FA_t + l_3 GDP_t - l_4 GI_{t-1} + \text{error}$$

where,

GI_t = government investment expenditure,
GR_t = government revenue,
FA_t = foreign assistance.

The inclusion of GDP and previous years public investment indicates that it captures acceleration principle and the influence of on-going projects for which commitments have already been made respectively.

The fourth and fifth components of aggregate demand function are the foreign sector. Turning to the export sector, exports are assumed to be a function of the real exchange rate and the level fo real output and foreign income. Thus, the export function may be expressed in the following form:

$$X_t = a_0 + a_1 e^t \frac{P_t^*}{P_t} + a_2 Y_t^* + a_3 GDP_t + a_4 X_{t-1}$$

where, Y_t^* = foreign income.

The lagged dependent variable incorporates the practical adjustment and $a_1>0$, $a_2>0$.

Imports

Real imports are related negatively to the real exchange rate and positively to real domestic product. The imports are generally dependent on the level of economic activity and development projects, foreign aid and grants and the level of purchasing power. Again to capture the practical adjustment behaviour a lag import term is included in the estimated equation. Similarly, restricted foreign exchange availability frequently leads to the imposition of import control and foreign exchange rationing, which act as a constraint on imports in developing countries like Nepal. Therefore, the reserve import ratio is also often included in the regression.

Thus, the import equation can therefore be written as:

$$Z_t = \delta_0 + \delta_1 \frac{e^t P_t^*}{P_t} + \delta_2 GDP_t + \delta_3 \frac{R_{t-1}}{P_{t-1}^* Z_{t-1}} + \delta_4 Z_{t-1}$$

where, R_t = foreign exchange value of international reserves.

Aggregate Supply Model

Let us consider the Cobb-Douglas production function relating labour and capital to output.

$$Y_t = \alpha_0 K^{\acute{a}1} L^{\acute{a}2}$$

where, K and L are the measures of the aggregate capital stock and labour respectively

α_1 and α_2 are the coefficient to be estimated.

In underdeveloped countries like Nepal, the estimation of the supply side of the model is hampered by the shortage of data on aggregate capital stock. Therefore, Haque adopted the following procedure:

Now taking the difference equation

$$K_t = (1 - \delta) K_{t-1} + I_t$$

where δ is the rate of depreciation.

Taking log in both sides we get,

$$\text{Log } K_t = \log \left[\sum_{i=0}^{t-1} (1-\delta)^I I_{t-1} + (1-\delta)^t K_0 \right]$$

where K_0 is the initial capital stock.

Adopting the log approximation, we obtain,

$$\text{Log } K_t = \log_2 + \frac{1}{2} \left[\log \sum_{i=0}^{t-1} (1-\delta)^i I_{t-1} + (1-\delta)^t K_0 \right]$$

$$\text{Log } K_t = \log_2 + \frac{1}{2} \log \sum_{i=0}^{t-1} (1-\delta)^i I_{t-1} + \frac{t}{2} \log (1-\delta)^t + \frac{1}{2} K_0$$

Thus, $\log Y_t = \log \alpha_0 + \alpha_1 \log K_t + \alpha_2 \log L_t$

$\log Y_t = \log \alpha_0 +$

$$\alpha_1 \left[\log 2 + \frac{1}{2} \log \sum_{i=0}^{t-1} (1-\delta) i \, I_{t-1} + \frac{t}{2} \log (1-\delta) + \log K_0 \right] + \alpha_2 \log L$$

The equation can be estimated for different values of δ over the interval (0, 1). By assuming constant returns to scale, the above equation can be written with the assumption of complete wage flexibility where the price wage flexibility in developing countries is an unsettled question. So, under the circumstances, the following empirical production function with lagged adjustment and technical progress over time as additional explanatory variables in per capita terms represents the economy's supply function:

$$\log (Y/L) = \log \alpha_0 + \alpha_1 \left[\log 2 + \frac{1}{2} \log \sum_{i=0}^{t-1} (1-\delta) i \, I_{t-1} + \right.$$

$$\left. \frac{t}{2} \log (1-\delta) + \frac{1}{2} \log K_0 \right] + \log L_t + g_t + \alpha_3 \log (Y/L)_{t-1} + \text{error}$$

The Nepalese Perspective

Agriculture Sector

Using the Cobb-Douglas type production function the model for agricultural sector is assumed to take real value added in this sector. Thus, the model be expressed as

$$\text{Log } VAA_t = a_0 + a_1 \log LAEA_t + a_2 \log GCL_t + a_3 \log PIL_t + \text{error}$$

where,

VAA_t = value added in agriculture,
$LAEA_t$ = labour employed in agriculture,
GCL_t = gross cultivated land,
PIL_t = proportion of irrigated land.

Industrial Sector

Nepalese economy is still behind in the development of industrial sector. There are some industries which contribute small proportion of total output and employment. Most industries are agro-based. So, to analyze the effect on industrial sector, the agricultural production is added in order to reflect the dependence of agro-based industries on agricultural inputs. Thus, the model for industrial sector would assume to be,

$$\text{Log } VAIS_t = b_0 + b_1 \log LFIS_t + b_2 \log KSIS_t + b_3 \log AGDP_t + \text{error.}$$

where,

$VAIS_t$ = value added in industrial sector,
$LFIS_t$ = labour force in industrial sector,
$KSIS_t$ = capital stock in industrial sector,
$AGDP_t$ = agriculture gross domestic product.

Social Service Sector

In this sector, Cobb-Douglas type production function is assumed to be

$$\text{Log } VAS_t = C_0 + C_1 \log LS_t + C_2 \log KS_t + C_3 GDP_t + \text{error}$$

where,

VAS_t = Value added in social services,
LS = Labour force in social services,

KS = Capital stock in social services.

In short, when modeling for Nepalese economy, the production block tentatively will have the eight major sectors. They can be modeled as,

$$VA_x = f(x\text{-}I)$$

where,

VA_x = value added in Xth sector,

x_i = Cumulative investment in Xth sector,

i = lag period, and

X = f (agriculture, Construction, Manufacturing and mining, Social services, Finance, real estate and dwelling, Transport and communication, trade and restaurant, and electricity, gas and water).

Money Supply and Price Block

The supply of money in the economy consists of reserves and domestic credit. The money supply function is dependent on the domestic credit, government fiscal deficit and foreign exchange reserves. In dealing with the money supply and prices block there are four major empirical models to be used for Nepalese economy :

1. $MS_t = a_0 + a_1 DC_t + a_2 GD_{t-1} + a_3 FER$ + error.

where,

MS_t = Money supply,

DC_t = Domestic credit,

GD_t = Government fiscal deficit, and

FER = Foreign exchange reserves.

2. $AGDP_t = b_0 + b_1 MS_t + b_2 INPI_{t-1}$ + error

where,

$AGDP_t$ = Agriculture GDP deflater,

$IMPI_t$ = Import price index.

3 $NAGDP_t = c_0 + c_1 MS_t + c_2 IMPI_{t-1}$ + error,

where, $NAGDP_t$ = Non-agriculture GDP deflator.

4. $CPI_t = d_0 + d_1 AGDPD_t + d_2 NAGDPD_t$ + error,

where, CPI_t = Consumer price index.

Now, turning to the money demand function, the demand for money is taken to be related relatively to the nominal rate of interest and positively to the level of income. Thus,

$$\text{Log}\,(M_T/P_t) = \alpha_0 + \alpha_1 I_t + \alpha_2 \log Y_t + \alpha_3 \log Y_{t-1} + \alpha_4 \log (M_{t-1}/P_{t-1}) + \text{error},$$

where,

(M_T/P_t) = Demand for money,

I_t = Nominal interest rate.

The lagged term in Y allows for different speeds of adjustment of the demand for money to changes in interest rates and income.

The Government Revenue Block

The main source of government revenue are the tax as well as non-tax revenue. These sources are divided into six major headings. The models to be used in government revenue sector are as follows:

1. $IT_t = a_0 + a_1 VAM_t + a_2 GDP_t + a_3 IT_{t-1}$ + error

   where, IT_t = income tax revenue,

   VAM_t = Value added in manufacturing.

   The inclusion of endogenous variable as an explanatory variable one period lag is to capture the partial adjustment responses.

2. $EXD_t = b_0 + b_1 VAM_t + b_2 GDP_t$ + error

   where, EXD_t = Excise duties.

3. $TAD_t = c_0 + c_1 IMG_t + c_2 TAD_{t-1}$ + error

   where, TAD = Tariff duties,

   IMG = Import of goods.

4. $SAT_t = d_0 + d_1 NAGDP_t + d_2 SAT_{t-1}$ + error

   where, SAT = Sales tax revenue.

5. $NTR = \alpha_0 + \alpha_1 NAGDP_t$ + error

   where, NTR = non-tax revenue.

6. $AGT_t = \alpha_0 + \alpha_1 TCA_t$ + error

   where, AGT_t = Agricultural tax,

   TCA_t = total cultivated land.

Labour Employment Block

There are tentatively nine sectors where the total labour force is engaged. The functional relationship between employment and these sectors can be expressed in the equation form as,

$$LX = f(VAX)$$

where,

LX = Employment in Xth sector,

VAX = Value added in Xth sector,

X = f (Agriculture, Construction, Tourism, Manufacturing and mining, Social services, Finance, real estate and dwelling, Transport and communication, trade and restaurant, and electricity, gas and water).

Validation of the Model

The R^2, DW, F and t statistics examine the estimates obtained from OLS which gives the statistical significance of the OLS estimates of the single equation model. But in the simultaneous system, it is necessary to evaluate the fitness of the multi-equation model, which is a precondition for examining the forecasting ability of the model. The application of OLS in the multi-equation model provides the inconsistent, bias and inefficient estimates. So, it is necessary to apply ILS method for the exactly identified simultaneous equation and 2 SLS and 3 SLS for the over identified simultaneous equation. For the accuracy of the estimates, which are estimated from the ILS, 2 SLS and 3 SLS the Cocrane-Orcutt iterative method and DW statistics are not the proper statistics to be used for the evaluation of accuracy of forecasts. Therefore, there are most common methods of perspective accuracy that have been used in the literature are Theil's Inequality Coefficient, Mean Square Error (MSE) and Root Mean Square Error (RMSE).

Theil's Index

Henry Theil has suggested a systematic measure of the accuracy of forecasts of the above econometric models. This measure is called the inequality coefficient and is defined by the expression

$$U^2 = \frac{\Sigma\left(P_i - A_j\right)/n}{\Sigma A_i^2/n}$$

where, P_i = predicted change in the dependent variable,
A_i = Actual change with dependent variable.

The smaller the value of the inequality coefficient, better will be the fit of the simulation. The value of U ranges from zero to infinity.

MSE and RMSE

The accuracy of the predictive performance where the purpose of the model is conditional prediction, the choice of technique has been based on the predictive performance of the estimates obtained from the various techniques. When attempting the ranking of the technique the most common measure of the forecasting performance has been the mean square error of the forecast or its square root. Thus,

$$MSE = \frac{\Sigma\left(F_i - A_j\right)^2}{n}$$

and,
$$RMSE = \sqrt{\frac{\Sigma\left(F_i - A_j\right)^2}{n}}$$

The accuracy of the aforesaid model can be evaluated by using above three indices.

Conclusion

In seeking solutions for various planning and policy issues of economic development, quantitative tools have been used widely. Macro-models influenced by Keynesian Income Expenditure theory are often to readdress short term stabilization problems. However, no consensus among policy makers in developing countries exists due to widespread differentiations remained in the socio-economic conditions and banking practices. On the basis of prevailing macro-economic conditions of the country, various models such as investment function, government investment expenditure, trade-imports and exports, industrial and agricultural sectors, services sector and models governing monetary aspects and revenue have been introduced. Most of the models include lag endogenous variable as an explanatory variable to capture the partial adjustments.

This paper attempted to fill a void in empirical Nepalese macro-economics. Most of the models include lag endogenous variable as an explanatory variable in order to capture the partial adjustment. The application of OLS in such circumstances will provide inaccurate, inconsistent and bias estimates. So, the suitable method to estimate the parameters stated in the models in simultaneous equation method. By the application of this method the accuracy of forecasts can be judged by using Theil's inequality index and Root Mean Square error as defined in the text.

3.2 PROJECT APPRAISAL IN DEVELOPING COUNTRIES*

The origin of the cost benefit can be traced back to the welfare economics of 19th century. It's first practical application began in United States of America in order to analyze the net benefit of water sources in 1930s. The concept of cost benefit now-a-days have become popular in analyzing the acceptance or rejection of a particular project with respect to social cost-benefit analysis. There are two methods of social cost benefit analysis which are popularly known as the Little/Marrlees and UNIDO methods. The major differences between these two approaches to social cost-benefit analysis can be visualized in selecting the numeraire to be used. The former method is based on the border price and accounting rate of interest based on public saving as numeraire while the latter is based on the domestic currencies and consumption rate of interest as numeraire. However, both the

* Modified from the original paper published in The Economic Journal of Nepal, Vol. 21, No. 4, 1998, pp. 171-79.

approaches have several evidences that the social cost benefit of a particular project gives similar results. This article aims to analyze the major components of the cost benefit analysis particularly on the basis of aforesaid two approaches.

Identifying Costs and Benefits

The identification of flow involved in project investment appraisal should be made as: initial period, investment cost; operating cost; the value of output; and the life of the project.

The value of the flow must then be discounted to obtain their present value as everything has an opportunity cost. Once the identification of net flow has been determined, the net present value (NPV) can be obtained through the discounted rate.

This is termed as the first profitability of the particular project. For social project appraisal, costs include all payments that reduce the availability of real resources to other user and benefit occurs when the project supplies additional goods or service or reduce the cost of goods previously available [*Roemer*, 1975].

Net Present Value (NPV)

The net present value criterion is based on the difference between benefits and costs, both discount rates in order to arrive at the NPV. These four basic steps are; the project costs and the benefits must be properly identified; once identified, the costs and benefits must be given a value reflecting market prices to asses private investors prospects and social prices to help to determine a government decision; costs and benefits must be compiled over time; and once the effects of time have been incorporated, benefits must be related to costs for each project so that projects can be compared to each other.

Once the above conditions are fulfilled, NPV can be measured as the Present Value of Benefits (PVB) less the Present Value of Costs (PVC), which the benefits and costs are, discounted at Minimum Return Requirement [MRR] or the opportunity costs rate of return of the resources employed in the project. In order to compute present value and appropriate discount rate is required.

The rate to be used is the MRR, which a public investment is required to earn if it is to be worthwhile. Unless the project is capable of earning this rate of return or something being discounted at this discount rate, the resources it uses should be better employed as an alternative use. If all future benefits and costs have been expressed in terms of present value with an appropriate discount rate, they can be added to find the NPV of the project. Three important points should be kept in mind when dealing with the NPV.

Firstly, the present value is always less than the nominal value that occurs in the future.

Secondly, the longer the delay in realizing some nominal value, the less is its present value, and

Lastly, the higher the interest rate the lower the present value.

As stated above, the first acceptability condition of the project is NPV. Acceptability required that NPV >0. (*Annex 1*).

Benefit Cost Ratio

The benefit cost ratio was for a time the most popular decision rule used in social project appraisal. The B/C ratio is measured as PVB/PVC again discounting at the MRR. In other words, it is calculated by dividing the sum of a project' discounted benefit by the sum of its discounted loss. It is the second criterion to accept or reject the project under consideration. The acceptability requires if the ratio is above 1. It means B/C>1.

Internal Rate Of Return (IRR)

It is that rate of discount applied to benefit and cost streams which sets PVB = PVC or NPV=0. The NPV and IRR both should be taken together when projects are being considered one at a time. These two methods are closely related. In calculating the NPV one can independently choose a discount rate based on the cost of capital and then found the difference between discounted benefits and costs. On the other hand the calculation of IRR reverses the procedure. Instead of selecting the discount rate one can set the NPV at zero and try to solve for discount rate. The process of finding the IRR is trial and error. (*Roemer* 1975). If the result is positive a higher rate is used, if negative a lower rate is used and the process is repeated until the NPV is reduced to zero. Thus, the discount rate that yields a zero net present value is the Internal Rate of Return (IRR). If the discount rate used in NPV is less than the social discount rate i.e. the value of IRR, the project under consideration is worthwhile, (*Pearce* 1971). If there are many projects having the same NPV, it will create a simple problem, i.e. which project should be selected? In such a situation, the B/C ratio should be marked which gives reasonable answer to choose a single project from amongst the various projects.

The Social Rate Of Discount

The choice of social rate of discount depends on the numeraire taken. The discount rate on the UNIDO method is Consumption Rate of Interest (CRI). Empirical study for CRI has some complications. The UNIDO approach is based on the bottom up on the basis of switching values. In this method one should convert the value of all inputs and outputs into their consumption equivalents. Switching value is the value at which a project becomes acceptable. The switching value of the project is the value of CRI that leaves a zero NPV for the project. It is the discount rate at which the NPV switches from positive to negative. Therefore, switching value can also be regarded as the IRR of the project. When more than one project is being considered, the switching value of the CRI is the discount rate at which one alternative comes to have a higher NPV than the other.

Similarly, the choice of numeraire in Little/Mirrless system is the public saving for the reason that the appropriate discount rate is the rate, in which the marginal utility of public saving falls. This rate is termed as he Accounting Rate of Interest (ARI) (*Thirlwall* 1994). If the too low ARI is chosen there will be excessive investment, a balance of payment deficit and underuse of resources (*Baldwin* 1972). The ARI should be kept as high as possible, consistent with their being as much investment as savings permits. (*Little/Mirrless* 1974). They suggested that most developing countries ought to use the rate around 10 per cent in real terms. They also suggest three rates for ARI: high, low and medium.

Shadow Prices

In order to compare the social costs and benefits of a project, it is necessary to value both the resources—factors of production used and the goods and services produced. The prices actually observed in the economy may not measure social value correctly. Whenever there are controls, monopoly power, administered or legislative prices, external economies and other market distortions, market prices will diverge from social opportunity costs and cannot be used in social project appraisal. Also, taxes and subsidies will introduce a spread between the prices consumers pay and those producers receive. In all these situations observed market prices must be adjusted or the correct market prices should be selected to reflect social values. These adjusted or selected prices are called shadow or social prices.

Theoretically, all shadow prices should be derived from a comprehensive mathematical model of the economy. In practice, however, shadow prices should be done selectively in terms of two criteria: *firstly*, the resources which figure most prominently in benefits and costs in market prices, and *secondly*, all resources unvalued in the project for which market prices are farthest out of reach compared to their respective shadow prices. Both these criteria must be applied simultaneously for determining the shadow prices. Having these two conditions in mind one can assess the basis of shadow prices, which are: main outputs; importable material inputs; major non-importable material inputs, and unskilled labour.

Once the basis of the shadow pricing are incorporated in the model, the fundamentals of shadow pricing should be evaluated. The most commonly used fundamentals of shadow prices are: the concept of tradability; the sources of shadow prices; the treatment of taxes; the choice of numeraire, and the use of adjustment factor.

Determination Of Shadow Prices

The UNIDO method clearly guides to determine the shadow price is the resources used by the project. In a perfect market the shadow price would be the market price. But in the real world, the marginal cost of production will be equal to the marginal price that consumers will be willing to pay for one more unit. It happens to the reason of the market imperfections, as tariffs, quotas and monopolies create distortions on demand and supply. There is little chance that market price reflect the true economic value and cost of inputs and outputs. For tradable resources the domestic market price is likely to be higher than the border price. Similarly, because of market distortions, marginal social cost as seen from the supply side for non-traded goods will also probably not be equal. Therefore, it is necessary to decide whether the project impacts were in demand and supply to determine shadow prices.

Realizing the above facts, project evaluator has to assess the impacts whether they are in demand or supply or both. The UNIDO method clearly recommends three sources of shadow prices depending on the project impact in national economy. These are:

- A project through its use and production of resources may for any given input or output affect the supply available to the rest of the economy; level of its production to the rest of the economy; level of its imports or exports.
- In terms of production of an output the project may: increase total consumption in the economy; decrease production in other parts of the economy; decrease imports or increase exports.
- The corollary impacts of the projects consumption may be; to decrease consumption of the rest of the

economy; to increase production within the economy; to increase imports or decrease exports.

Therefore, while determining the shadow price of resources, the sources of shadow pricing must be assessed by taking the impacts on the whole economy after which the project is to be acceptable.

The Unique Feature Of Developing Countries And Shadow Exchange Rate

Most of the under-developed countries are typical; Industries have not developed the capacity to supply most of the capital and intermediate goods required for continued development. So, most of the developing countries like Nepal will critically depend on imports. The capacity to earn or save foreign exchange will, therefore, remain a critical concern of development plans and policies. Having this environment, foreign exchange becomes a factor of production, because it represents ability to purchase capital equipment, industrial or agriculture inputs and consumer necessities. Realizing the above facts, the currencies of developing countries are drastically overvalued. The official rate is undervalued to that of market exchange rate. In other words, the official rate of foreign exchange is likely to remain below the market rate of exchange. Therefore, shadow price for foreign exchange should be considered when the appraisal of projects are to be undertaken.

Shadow Wage Rate

Most of the labour used in any sector comes from a labour surplus rural sector and its departure involves a little or no loss of agricultural production, i.e. the opportunity cost equal to its marginal productivity is typically very low. (*Baldwin* 1972). However, the wage rate of labour used in other sectors of economy rather than in the agricultural sector, will be determined above the wage rate of agricultural sector, due to the pressure of trade unions. Therefore, in such circumstances, the actual wage rate lies between the actual market wage rate and agriculture subsistance wage rate, which is known as the shadow wage of the labour. There are other impacts such as in distribution and income, the evaluation of such impacts are beyond the scope of this article.

Adjustment Or Conversion Factors

The financial values found in the financial tables must be transformed into economic values, which indicate the premium, and that must be added or the discount that must be subtracted to reflect the difference between financial and economic values.

The adjustment factors used in the UNIDO analysis are closely related to well-known conversion factors or accounting ratios in the Little/Mirrless analysis. According to them the actual prices paid cover the cost of imported inputs including import duties, the market cost of various other inputs, the cost of labour at the ruling wage rates, profit and tax payments. To get the accounting price of the inputs, of the ruling wage rates, it would like to subtract import duties and other indirect taxes, the excess of profits over that required to cover the ARI and to add on some allowance for the consumption out of profits by those involved in providing the services. This is hard work, so, instead the project evaluator can take some average of the ratios of accounting prices to market prices. These ratios are called conversion factors. The adjustment factor in UNIDO analysis is equal to the conversion factor minus unity.

Conclusion

Most of the developing countries are handicapped by the proper investment decision guidance's. The investment decisions should be guided by above discussed cost and benefit measurements. This measuring instrument for social cost benefit analysis is used in public as well as private investment decisions in order to rationalize the guidelines for investment in which specific use of inputs with alternative uses should be determined to the optimum possible scale. To obtain this goal of investments, the task that confronts us is to develop a consistent and generally acceptable set of weights that will select just those projects that will yield the maximum benefits for a given expenditure of public funds. For this reason, project appraisal is a technique that permits us to derive such a set weights or prices.

3.3 MEASURE OF INEQUALITY: ILLUSTRATIONS FROM NEPALESE HEALTH SECTOR*

Inequality refers to the situation in which the particular variable under investigation does not show equality. The citizens of UDC's and DC's are suffering from economic inequalities as well. Many economic variables such as income, wealth, tax, land, import, export, education, health, regional development etc. are not distributed proportionally. The problem of equal distribution of variables under consideration is more acute in UDC's and DC's. Such disparities in the distribution of the variables can be measured by taking the different groups of people or different geographical areas. A technical note of the methods of measuring inequality is briefly summarized as follows:

The first measure of inequalities is Coefficient of Variation (V). It is the easiest method to measure inequality. The coefficient of variation is defined as the ratio of standard deviation to the mean value of the investigation variable under question:

$$V = \frac{\sigma}{\overline{X}}$$

where,

V = Coefficient of variation,

σ = Standard Deviation,

$\overline{X}$ = Arithmetic mean.

The second measure of inequality is the concentration index (c). The method to calculate the concentration index is:

* *Modified from the original paper published in The Economic Journal of Nepal, Vol. 15, No. 2, 1992, pp.46-51*

$$C = \frac{V}{2}$$

where, C= Concentration index,

$$V = \frac{\bar{d}}{\bar{x}}$$

and,

$$\bar{d} = \frac{1}{n}\sum_{i=1}(x_i - \bar{x}_i)$$

The third measure of inequality is the Gini coefficient (G.C.) named after the Italian statistician. The Gini coefficient is the difference between the absolute equality line and Lorenj curve of the two distributions. Therefore, Gini coefficient is exactly one half of the relative mean difference defined as the Arithmetic mean of the pairs of income divided by mean income.

This method of measuring inequality is very important because, it is widely accepted and used. It presents, the concentration ratio between Lorenz curve and absolute equality line. So, Gini coefficient is the ratio of the area between diagonal and the curve to the area of the triangle below the diagonal. This can be illustrated with the help of the diagram.

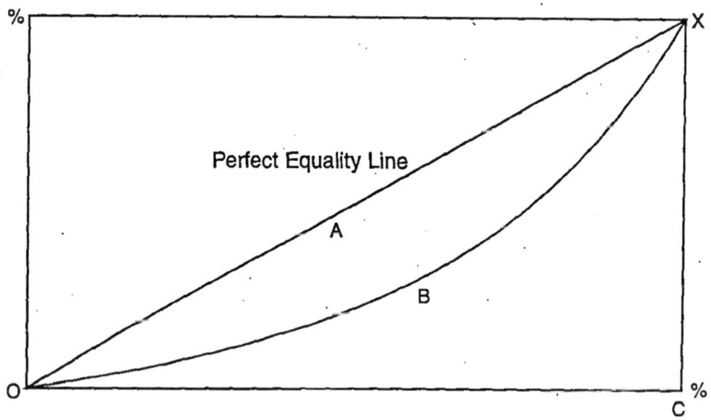

Fig. 1. Perfect Equality Line

The line OX is the absolute equality line, which is based on the 45^0 lines. The lower part of the curve is known as the Lorenz curve, which is used to measure the inequality of variables under consideration. In other words the purpose of this curve is to show the degree of equality in the relevant distribution wherefrom it is taken. Now, the area between Lorenz curve and absolute equality line is denoted by A which is called the concentration area of the inequality and the area of the triangle (O X C) below the diagonal is denoted by B

$$\therefore \qquad \text{G.C.} = \frac{A}{A+B}$$

It means Gini coefficient is the ratio of the concentration area (A) to the area below the absolute equality line A+B.

From the above fact it is found that the Gini coefficient is closely related with Lorenj curve. For the construction of Lorenz curve the cumulative percentage share of variables under investigation and the population is needed. These units have first to be ordered according to the ratio of advantage. For Gini coefficient few clear methods of calculation are available in the literature. But it is easy if the value needed for the construction of Lorenz curve have already been calculated. Practically, Gini coefficient can be calculated by using the following formula for individual and group data:

From individual data

$$\text{G.C.} = \frac{1}{2n^2\mu}\sum_{I=1}^{n}\sum_{j=1}^{n}(y_i - y_j)$$

$$= 1 + \frac{1}{n} - 2/n^2\mu(y_1 + 2y_2 + ... + = ny_n)$$

where,

n = number of observation,

μ = mean value of y

and for $(y_1 \geq y_2 \geq .... \geq y_n)$

From the group data:

$$G = \Sigma\, x_i y_{i+1} - \Sigma\, x_{i+1}\, y_i$$

where

x_i = the cumulative proportion of x variable in the

ith class interval,

y_i = cumulative proportion of y variable in the ith class interval.

If x_i and y_i are considered as two columns the above equation can be rewritten as the sum of all the (n-1) determinate values of x_i and y_i taken two consecutive class intervals at a time. Thus,

$$\begin{bmatrix} x_i & y_i \\ x_{i+1} & y_{i+1} \end{bmatrix} \quad \text{for I = 1,2,3......, (n-1).}$$

As defined above the variables x and y should be measured in proportion not in the percentages. However, if these variables are calculated as percentages, each of them have to be divided by 100. In this case the Gini coefficient will be calculated as,

$$G = 1/100\ [\Sigma\, x_i y_{i+1} - \Sigma\, x_{i+1}\, y_i] \text{ per cent.}$$

$$G = 1/(100)^2\ [\Sigma\, x_i y_{i+1} - \Sigma\, x_{i+1}\, y_i]$$

The theoretical basis of Gini coefficient is that the value of Gini coefficient lies between 0 and 1. If the value of the Gini coefficient is zero, there is the absolute equality of the distribution of variables under consideration and if the value of the Gini coefficient is one there are extreme inequalities of distribution of variables under investigation.

The Nepalese Health Services

Nepal is a unique country in which every sector of the economy is extremely paralyzed in the sense of development. These sectors are unable to meet the basic requirements of the people. The urban sector of Nepal is more developed than the rural one. The concentration of the human facilities, by virtue of the development centered within the urban areas. The inequalities of all the economic variables are inherited and being pushed to the Nepalese people into poverty. Social justice such as equal distribution of health, education and employment facilities could not be expected proportionately. The inadequacy of such basic needs always push the people under severe under-nourishment, which ultimately prevents to hard labour and hence people are inherited with poor health and education as well. The health service of an economy is one of the basic needs of the people. This sector is badly affected by the unjust distribution of physicians and other nursing persons due to the fact that most of the physicians are stationed in urban areas, the urban areas are not largely affected by the health facility. 1989 data show that one bed is available for 3872 people. The total number of doctors was 1196 in 1990/91 and one doctor is available for 1544 people (SPB: 1992). The article will evaluate and examine the inequalities of the distribution of health workers of Nepalese economy.

To analyze the inequalities in health services of Nepal, Gini coefficient alone is taken into consideration because it is the most widely used method of measuring inequalities of the variables under investigation as already said above. The variables such as hospitals, health centers, hospital beds and medical doctors are considered on the one hand and the zonal wise distribution of population on the other. The main theme of this article is to analyze the distribution of above-said variables with the zonal-wise distribution of population.

The following diagram shows the Lorenj curve of four indicators of medical services in Nepal.

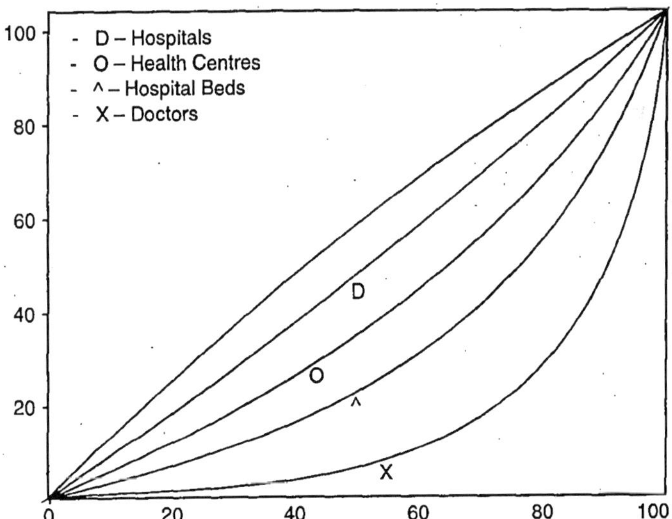

Fig. 2 Cumulative Percentage Share of variables under investigation (qi)

From the above curve it can be said that the hospitals are much more equally distributed than other variables under question. Another indicator of the availability of medical facilities, such that it is frequently employed and widely available is the number of hospital beds. The number of hospital beds is not evenly distributed with the proportion of the population in different regions of the country. Similarly, the doctors are not equally distributed in the different zones and the different regions of the country. Among the four indicators, the most wide uneven distribution can be seen on the part of doctors from the above figure.

Following are the values of the Gini coefficient of four indicators as explained above:

Based on (Year 1991)

Particulars	*Gini Coefficient in Percent*
Doctors	67.16
Hospital Beds	29.12
Health centers	16.91
Hospitals	4.64

The Gini coefficient of hospitals by taking the zonal wise distribution is 4.64 per cent. It means there is approximately equal distribution of hospitals in different zones of the country. The disparities in the number of health centers are greater than the hospitals but lesser than the hospital beds. The value of the Gini Coefficient is 16.91 per cent. These two indicators seem to be evenly distributed in different zones of the country.

Another indicator of the availability of the medical facilities frequently employed and widely available is the number of hospital beds. There is the moderate distribution of the number of hospital beds on the different zones of the country. The value of the Gini Coefficient is 29.12 per cent. It means only 29.12 per cent are the inequalities in the distribution of hospital beds. The fourth indicator is the distribution of medical doctors throughout the country. The value of Gini Coefficient is 67.13 per cent. It is found that among the four indicators of health services, the most uneven distribution of the doctors in different zones of the country is 67.16 per cent.

From the analysis of health services of Nepal, an amazing fact can easily be drawn about how much and where the medical facilities are concentrated. The hospitals, health centers, hospital beds to some extent, are evenly distributed in the different 14 zones of the country. But, the most important factor, which can be considered as the key player in health services game to operate these facilities, is the medical doctors whose distribution is extremely unequal as compared to other three indicators. This is the important reason for the poor health of the people in different regions, i.e., due to the poor distribution of doctors.

Mere existence of hospitals and health centers in different regions of the country does not by itself guarantee good health services. So, it is necessary to distribute the medical personnel equally in different regions of the country to serve the people and to operate other available facilities.

Finally, this being the situation of health services the hospitals and hospital beds are to some extent evenly distributed, but these facilities are virtually concentrated in the different urban centers of the country. In this context, the majority of the people reside in rural areas. The facility of having transport from rural areas to urban one is far from expectation in the existing condition. Therefore, the impact of these available facilities to the general health of people is being the fruits of sky.

Similarly, as stated above the distribution of doctors in regional basis is extremely uneven. This uneven distribution of physicians brought about a severe problem in the country. So, it deserves the attention that, only the hospitals and hospitals beds do not serve the general health of people, but equally it is necessary apparatus, incentive and facility to operate this apparatus. Special training programmes to doctors from the different remote regions of the country should also be introduced frequently. So, in this respect, the government should take care of meeting necessary apparatus and facilities to hospitals of different regions and the more important duty that the government should undertake is to distribute the medical personnel evenly in different regions of the country.

3.4 INPUT-OUTPUT MODEL WITH REFERENCE TO UNDER-DEVELOPED COUNTRIES*

With the pace of economic development and transformation of the mode of production, *classical economic theory* has remained as a theory that does not meet the requirements of the changing behaviour. Some economists of the pre-classical period attempted to focus on the problem of economic aggregation. The theoretical construction of the Tableau economique explored by Froncois Quency was a meaningful attempt. In 1874, Walras attempted to bring the *general equilibrium theory*, which constitutes the economy as a whole. But these theories remain only the showpieces of economic theories almost upto 1930s. At the same period the partial economic analysis failed to manipulate the economic variables. The complexity of economic problems of 1930s made the classical theory a failure. Since then many theories have been investigated by different economists to overcome the ever existing problems. The search for economic integration was the then present need. As a result, focuses have been made to study the production related relationship in the economy. Working on these lines W.W. Leontief has propounded the *input-output analysis* with a view to study the inter-dependence between the various industries with empirical analysis of production. This method of the studying relationship between various sectors of an economy is purely a mathematical orientation. The input-output analysis focuses its attention in general equilibrium of Walrasian type. It seeks to take account of the interdependence of the many industries/sectors, which constitute the economy:

(*i*) W.W. Leontief has specified a number of assumptions to make the input-output analysis simple. The

* Modified from the original paper published in The Economic Journal of Nepal, Vol. 11, No.4, 1988.

simplifying assumptions are the homogeneity of production, which requires perfect equilibrium and the production of any industry is subject to constant returns to scale. The basis of the input-output analysis is that every sector of an economy should use a fixed amount of input-output ratio on the one hand and the mathematical relationship can be specified in money terms on the other.

(ii) The input-output analysis has a great achievement in production planning. A planner can use input-output model to formulate short period plans. It shows the inter-dependence of the industries or sectors on the one hand and it predicts the quantities of production to meet the input requirement of the system and consumer requirements on the other. In a transaction table of an economy, if the household sector is simply treated as a consumption unit only, the analysis is called a static one. This article evaluates the static open model only.

(iii) *The model:* From the above analysis it is clear that to produce one unit of jth commodity the required ith input is constant and let us call it a_{ij}. The first subscript shows the input and second output.

Thus the production of each unit of the ith commodity would need say a_{ij}, a_{ij} and a_{nj} of the first, second and nth input.

Let us suppose that there are n^0 industries in the economy, concerning to n industries, the input-output table is in the form of the matrix A = $/a_{ij}/$ where a_{ij} would refer the input coefficients. Such a table shows the inter-industry dependence of flows within the economy. Each column of the table shows the necessary input for producing one unit of the output of certain industry. If any element in the matrix is zero, it shows that the input demand by that industry is zero.

From the above discussion the input coefficient can be written as:

$$a_{ij} = X_{ij} / X_j \ (i \ \& \ j = 1, 2, 3 \ ...... \ n)$$

where,

x_{ij} = total output of jth industry.

x_{ij} = number of units of ith good used as input by the jth industry.

a_{ij} = input coefficients.

The input-output mp3
table usually can be given as:

TABLE 1
Input-output Table

Input	Output I	II	III	n	Final demand
I	a_{11}	a_{12}	a_{13}	a_{1n}	d_1
II	a_{21}	a_{22}	a_{23}	a_{2n}	d_2
III	a_{31}	a_{32}	a_{33}	a_{3n}	d_3
–	.....	.....	....	....	....
...	......	.....	....	....	....
n	a_{ni}	a_{n2}	a_{n3}	a_{nn}	d_n

The above table shows the inter-industry dependence. Each column of this table specifies the input requirement for the production of one unit of a particular commodity. The second column states that to produce a unit of commodity[2], the inputs needed is a_{12} units of commodity, $^1a_{22}$ unit of commodity and so on. Dividing the produced and factor inputs of each industry by its output level compute average input-output coefficients. The sum of the column entries for and industry, and the column sums of the coefficients equal 1. Therefore, the column sums of coefficients for produced will be less than one.[3]

Symbolically, it can be shown as,

$$\sum_{j=i}^{n} a_{ij} < 1. \qquad (j = 1,2................n)$$

It follows that the value of primary input required to produce a unit of jth good is given by

$$1 - \sum_{j=I}^{n} a_{ij}$$

From the input-output table given above we can easily

derive the following equation:

$$X_1 = a_{11} * 1 + a_{12} *2 + a_{13} *3 + \ldots\ldots\ldots\ldots a_{1n} * n + d_1$$
$$X_2 = a_{21} * 1 + a_{22} *2 + a_{23} *3 + \ldots\ldots\ldots\ldots a_{2n} * n + d_2$$
$$X_3 = a_{31} * 1 + a_{32} *2 + a_{33} *3 + \ldots\ldots\ldots\ldots a_{3n} * n + d_3$$

....

....

$$X_n = a_{n1} * 1 + a_{n2} *2 + a_{n3} *3 + \ldots\ldots\ldots\ldots a_{nn} * n + d_n.$$

The above system of equation can be written in the matrix form as,

$$(I\text{-}A)\,X = \begin{bmatrix} -a_{11} & a_{12} & -a_{13}\ldots\ldots -a_{1n} \\ -a_{21} & 1-a_{22} & -a_{23}\ldots -a_{2n} \\ -a_{31} & a_{32} & 1-a_{33}\ldots -a_{3n} \\ --- & --- & --- \\ --- & --- & --- \\ a_{n1} & -a_{n2} & -a_{n3}\ldots 1-a_{nn} \end{bmatrix} \begin{bmatrix} X_1 \\ X_2 \\ X_3 \\ \cdot \\ \cdot \\ X_n \end{bmatrix} = \begin{bmatrix} d_1 \\ d_2 \\ d_3 \\ \cdot \\ \cdot \\ d_n \end{bmatrix}$$

where,

I = identity matrix of order n.
A= input coefficient matrix of order n.
X = unknown variables to be determined.
d = final demand vector.

Now , solving for X we have,

$$X_i = (I - A)^{-1}d.$$

Under-developed Countries and Input-output Model

Most of the UDC's are characterized by many technological and economic problems. Market imperfections in such countries led to the dualistic pattern of the economy. The dualistic pattern of development divides the country into two main sectors. Some of the urban centers of the country are well-developed whereas the rural sectors are fully guided by the primitive pattern of development. In such economies, the modern as well as traditional methods of production are operating side by side. The urban sector of the economy uses the modern method, and in the rural sector the case is reverse. The primitive method of production in UDC's leads to low level of productivity and income. So, in these economies, the coexistence of technologies have made the features within a meaningful theoretical framework and has raised many methodological issues. To sum up the problem most of the kinds, which render the price mechanism ineffective as an allocative device, with the economy being divided into segregated regions having a vast non-monetized sector and limping price system. The inter-connections of various sectors in fact has not well developed. The inter-dependence of various industries can be evaluated either by consumption or through technology. The investment pattern in such economies has made complications to classify the input from the final consumption. Diversification of the pattern of development have made more obstacles to find out the interdependence of the industries.

As in the calculation of national income the double counting of goods is possible within the system. The input-output model as stated above is the empirical calculation of production activities. So, it is necessary to avoid the possibilities of double counting of goods of each and every sector of an economy. Similarly, in these societies, the more difficult challenging task is to distinguish final, intermediate and primary goods. Because "Input-output analysis traces the flow of production in order to study the effects of a change in the demand for final goods on production of primary, intermediate and final goods."

The under-developed countries are characterized by such problems. Due to the dualistic pattern of production system, it is one of the vivid complications to distinguish the primary, intermediate and final goods in UDC's. So, it is necessary to distinguish between the primary, intermediate and final goods within the economic system.

In UDC's the economy is segregated into many sectors. These sectors are operated, to some extent, independently. Micro level study is possible in such a society. To transfer the particular sector into aggregation in such societies is a challenging problem. From the above point of view, it becomes more difficult to study the general empirical equilibrium analysis. So, "the practical difficulties of efficient utilization and interpretation of large amounts of detailed qualitative information constituted the principal obstacle in the path of the development of general empirical analysis. The only possible way of overcoming the resulting impasse seemed to point towards the *detour* via aggregative analysis. So, one has to give detailed attention to concentrate the economic system from micro level to macro level. For such works in UDC's, the number of simplifying assumption has to be made in order to get the general empirical equilibrium.

As stated above, the economy of UDC's is fully operated by the dualistic pattern. In these economies, the pace of monetization is low. It will counter the system as a whole. So, due to lack of monetization, it is very difficult to distinguish between the input that is used by industry itself and when sells it as an input to other industries. How much produce has been used to meet the requirements of consumers is another aspect to be faced in such societies. Without the monetary measurement, one cannot forecast the situation as to how much is produced in the economy and where the produced goods are distributed among the industries and consumers and what is the quantity. To solve these questions the economy as a whole should be monetized on the one hand and all the input-output used and produced by each sector should be counted in money terms on the other. So, monetization and market perfection of the economy becomes the primary function for the study of the general empirical equilibrium analysis.

Another major problem in constructing the input-output table of UDC's is the lack of statistical information. It is very difficult to obtain sufficient information about the economic activities in such societies. Due to the dual system of production pattern, different technologies have been used to produce the goods. The large and small scale of production in urban and rural sector of an economy does not provide the clear picture as required by the system. In this situation, it is very difficult to classify the goods that are for final consumption and for the use of final requirement. For instance, it can be said that the collected information will not provide sufficient material to such model. So, one has to develop the new technique and methodology to collect the information in UDC's. The purposewise production information is regarded as the main source of data.

Finally, even though there are so many problems in the path of the construction of input-output table in UDC's, it has become one of the main tool of planning. Many UDC's of the world have been preparing input-output tables to study the production activities within the economy. Now-a-days, this technique has the main application in the field if production planning. So, in order to formulate the economic planning in UDC's, one can use the input-output table easily.

Annexure 1

Once all future benefits and costs have been expressed in terms of present values, they can be added to find the net present value (NPV) of the project. Thus,

$$NPV = \frac{B_0 - C_0}{(1+i)^t} + \frac{B_1 - C_1}{(1+i)} + \frac{B_2 - C_2}{(1+i)^2} + \ldots$$

$$+ \frac{Bt - Ct}{(1+i)^t} + \ldots + \frac{Bn - Cn}{(1+i)^n}$$

where,

Bt = total benefits in year t.
Ct = total cost in year t.
Bt-Ct = net benefit in year t.
I = discount interest rate.
n = number of years, duration of the project.

Note that NPV may be positive or negative .

Similarly, we can obtain the basic equation for the calculation of IRR as,

$$O = \frac{B_0 - C_0}{(1+i)^0} + \frac{B_1 - C_1}{(1+i)^1} + \frac{B_2 - C_2}{(1+i)^2} + \ldots + \frac{Bn - Cn}{(1+i)^n}$$

where the symbols have the same meaning as above.

As stated in the main part of the article, the procedure for obtaining the IRR is iterative. Then, the simple iterative method of obtaining IRR is given by,

$$\text{IRR} = \frac{\text{lower discount rate} - \text{difference between the highest and lower discount rates} * \text{NPV at lower discount rate}}{\text{the difference of NPV at lower and higher discount rate}}$$

For the rejection/acceptance of the particular project the IRR does not provide the criterion for selection of projects. Thus, IRR should be compared with market rate of interest or social rate of interest. The procedure of comparisons is as follows:

If IRR is greater than the market interest rate or social rate of interest, then select the project under consideration. Now, taking the hypothetical example to find the NPV and IRR:

TABLE 2
Calculation of NPV & IRR

Years	*Total Cost*	*Total Benefits*	*Net Cash Flow*	*10% DF at*	*NPV*	*25% DF at*	*NPV*
1	100	–	–10	0.909	–90.9	0.800	-80.00
2	100	–	–100	0.826	–82.6	0.640	64.00
3	–	90	90	0.751	67.59	0.512	46.08
4	–	100	100	0.683	83.30	0.410	41.00
5	–	150	150	0.621	93.15	0.328	49.20
Total	200	340	140	–	70.54	–	–7.72

Here, NPV at 10 per cent is 70.54 >, thus the project is worthwhile, But the NPV at 25 per cent is –7.72. So, the project is not worthwhile. This example provides the basis for obtaining IRR.

$$\text{IRR} = 10 + 15 \left[\frac{70.54}{70.54 + 7.72}\right] \text{ 23 per cent}$$

Similarly, the discount factor (DF) = $\frac{1}{(1+i)^t}$.

Annexure 2

TABLE 1
Population, Number of Hospitals and Hospital Beds, Health Centres and Doctors by Zone.

Zone	*Population (in million)*	*Hospitals*	*Hospital Beds*	*Health Centers*	*Doctors*
Mechi	1.12	4	95	48	19
Koshi	1.73	10	348	81	63
Sagarmatha	1.59	8	282	72	29
Janakpur	2.06	8	167	81	28
Bagmati	2.25	24	2076	52	854
Narayani	1.87	8	420	68	42
Gandaki	1.26	7	340	96	49
Dhawalgiri	0.49	4	60	47	8
Lumbini	2.00	12	324	78	34
Rapti	1.04	5	110	54	7
Bheri	1.10	7	178	59	23
Karnali	0.26	1	15	54	6
Seti	1.03	8	243	70	21
Mahakali	0.66	5	110	49	13
Total	18.46	111	4768	919	1196

Source: Statistical Pocket Book 1992, Central Bureau of Statistics, Kathmandu. Ministry of Health, HMG/N, Kathmandu.

CHAPTER FOUR

The Political Economy

4.1 NEPAL'S DRIVE TOWARDS PRIVATIZATION*

The transfer of economic activities of a country from the public sector to private sector known as 'privatization' can take several forms. Generally, privatization is used to mean lesser control and regulation by the state in economic activities. The main technique of privatization is:

(i) To transfer the management of state enterprises through contract and lease.

(ii) To sale the share of public ownership enterprises to private sector.

(iii) To enhance and promote private sector in various lines of production.

(iv) To sell equity share of public companies to private sector.

Similarly, we can interpret privatization as denationalization, liberalization and deregulation. In the perspective of Nepalese context privatization comprises any of these forms. Since the past few years the government of Nepal has been making efforts to transfer economic activities from the public to the private sector. Broadly defined, 'privatization in Nepal is the denationalization of economic activities by promoting the

---

* Modified from the original paper published in The Economic Journal of Nepal, Vol. 12, No. 2, 1989.

national and multinational companies'. Inspite of these, economic privatization of Nepal aims to transfer some economic activities of the state to the private sector. Though the economic system as mentioned in the Constitution of Nepal and practiced over the years, operated through the mixed system. Given the nature of economic system and constitutional provisions it may be hard to do so. The economic activities of Nepal, at present, directly or indirectly, are regulated and operated by the state. But from the past few years, the Government of Nepal has been making efforts to mobilize the private sector in economic and social activities. Privatization (the transfer of the public activities to private sector) has been the focus point of this paper. It also tries to examine the major consequences of privatization in UDC's especially in Nepalese context.

HISTORICAL BACKGROUND OF PRIVATIZATION

In pre-World War II period, the world economy had been driven towards the private sector. Government control in the economic activities of the state had not been affective, the *laissez-fair doctrine* of economic philosophy was operated and formulated by Adam Smith. Nationalization of economic activities at the time was insignificant. Less control by the state in the economic activities had been regarded as the main thrust of economic goal. The great depression of 1930, especially in the western world, challenged the system of *laissez-fair doctrine* and numerous economic activities were stopped by the Government. Since then, the governments of the world have been forced to rethink over the free enterprises. After the great challenge of the failure of the free economic system, the world economy had to be revised and thought over the accepted classical economic doctrine. So, the newly freed as well as the rest of the nations as a result of the Second World War, with burning national feeling combined with the Keynesian doctrine. The post World War II period witnessed an enormous expansion of government intervention in national economy, particularly in the 1960's and early 1970s, when the public sector was seen as the major contributor to economic growth and socio-political stability. Since the beginning of 1980s the world economic system has changed its gear to the direction of free enterprise system. As a result of this, the world switched its speed from public to private control of the economic activities. The capitalist as well as mixed economy of the world have placed their action on privatization. Not only the capitalist and mixed economic system make practice of the privatization but also the socialist economic system is trying to exercise it. The fullest form of it is the so-called open policy of China and Perestroika in Russia. The denationalization and deregularization of economic activities of Britain also are burning examples of privatization.

Consequences Of Public Undertakings

The consequences of public ownership and operations of public enterprises may serve the group of national interest but it may not be able to serve the individual interest. Badly paid manager will not work to serve the interest of the economy as a whole. Exploitation may increase within the system. Politicians interfere with the operations of public enterprises. So these factors have combined to reduce the cost or production efficiency of public production, which is often leading to heavy dependence of budgetary support. In pursuing their personal goals politicians, managers and workers waterdown from higher priority objectives of public enterprises.[1]

1. From the past economic history, it is known that privatization of economic activities in Nepal is not new. Before 1950, the economic activities were run and operated by private sector, either it was individual effort or community level efforts. The economy of Nepal was confined to the private sector in which people produced goods and services for themselves. At that time they sold their surplus products in local markets. Besides this, people contributed some part of their production as tax to meet the governments administrative expenditure. The world has changed its momentum from private to public undertakings of economic activities when the great depression of 1930s had occurred. As a result of this the then Rana Regime of Nepal also introduced the Public Enterprises

From the above point of view, the capitalist countries of the world exercised the free enterprises system to serve the common interest of the people. The socialist countries of the world with planned development and state owned companies are trying to transfer the state owned activities in a slow speed gear to privatization. Similarly, the speeding up of the gear of privatization is not only in the capitalist and socialist countries of the world but also in the developing countries like India and Nepal[2], which are having the mixed economic system. Most of the developing countries are experiencing the mixed economic system owned by more public enterprises with vast revenue earning capacities. Public companies in any country whether it is developed or underdeveloped, create a natural monopoly due to several reasons. The natural monopoly may exist in such enterprises due to the soft and hard restrictions for entry and protective measure taken by the government. if such enterprises are left behind to the private sector, this type of monopoly will be limited. If the government does not have any obligation to restrict the entry.

Privatization is essentially an industrial country phenomenon. Public ownership of enterprise is the characteristic of developing countries. But since last few decades Nepal[3] had followed the mixed economic system. It has been controlling and regulating the economic activities.

Act of 1936. Since then the public ownership of economic activities took place slowly.

2. After marked change in 1951, Constitutional provision as mixed economy of Nepal was confining to both the public and private sector. As a result of the constitutional provision, the main thrust was given to public sector. Since then the economic system of Nepal has changed its momentum from private sector to public sector. So, it can be said that the change of Nepalese politics has brought the alarming reforms in economic structure of the country. Besides the government of Nepal made many efforts to develop the public undertakings.
3. Prior to the implementation of First Five Year plan (1956-61) the public enterprises were limited. With the initiation of planned development of Nepal, the economic activities had increased tremendously. During the first five-year plan seven public enterprises came into operation. During the second three-year plan

Nepal's Experience With Privatization

Nepal's economy is predominantly based on agriculture. Nepal has recently started to handover economic and social activities to the private sector. The following are the sectors, which are driven to privatization:

(a) Before implementation of New Education Plan in 1972, the educational institutions were run by private sector, but after the introduction of new Education Plan in the same year, all the institutions (school and colleges) were brought under government-control with autonomous body regarding higher education system.

The New Education Plan had certainly the quantities aspect but without any qualitative improvement. So, the New Education Plan failed without gathering any experience and the education system was geared back to the old system. Privatizing schools and colleges have two aspects:

Firstly, is the mobilization of local resources with local

(1962-65 A.D.) 11 public enterprises were established in consonance with the policy of the government to transfer government enterprises into autonomous public undertakings. Additional 12 and 27 public enterprises were established in the period of third and fourth plans respectively. So, by July 1975, there were already 61 public enterprises in operation in the country. However, the large number of such undertakings meant duplication of activities and some of them were of little importance. Therefore, from 1975 onwards policies were taken to merge, consolidate, privatize and even to dissolve some of the enterprises. Accordingly, six enterprises were dissolved during the fifth five-year plan. But four new enterprises came into operation during this period. The number of total public enterprises remained 59 in 1979/80. This process continued during the sixth five-year plan (1980-85). During this period, six enterprises were dissolved whereas one new enterprise was established. Similarly, the public enterprises were established with 80 per cent share of government in the current seventh plan period. From these data the conclusion may be drawn that the economy is based on the public sector. From the past four decades it is seen that the private sector's role in economic activities is insignificant.

participation. People can establish schools and colleges by mobilizing their own resources for their own benefit.

Secondly, the government can transfer its economic responsibility of developing and expanding the education system to the private sector.

This process of privatizing the educational system has started from early 1980s. Since then, many private schools and colleges were opened and run by mobilizing the resources of private sector. But 80 per cent of these schools and colleges became bankrupt. So, the policy of government to privatize the schools and colleges does not seem effective.

(*b*) The forest sector has been an important sector under the private ownership from the very beginning. The government controlled some forest areas of the country. At that time the forest area was governed and controlled both by the government as well as the private sector. But since past few decades, the government has took control of all the forest land. As a consequence, the private sector has become inactive. The misuse of forest under the government control has increased alarmingly. So the forest depletion of the country increased in the past (one decade or more). Since few past years, the government of Nepal has taken policies to develop the forest by transferring the ownership to the private sector. Now-a-days the forest depletion of the country exceeds its limitation. So, the government of Nepal categories the forest area into three main parts. These three parts of forest area comprise of government owned, panchayat owned and private owned respectively.

(c) The banking sector is yet another area in which privatization is being proposed. The budget for fiscal year 1984/85 for the first time stressed on creating active participation of the people in the process of economic development. The trade and banking sectors are being privatized since the past few years. But these are not fully transferred to the private sector because the government has not withdrawn its share. The fully state owned trading company is National Trading Limited which limits its activities to import and export of goods. Because of liberalization of license system, private companies have increased their speed in export and import of goods.

These are the some major steps, which are being taken by the government of Nepal to transfer the state economic activities to the private sector. The banking sector of Nepal now gets some momentum and few of them are already established with the collaboration of foreigners. These multinational companies are selling their share to the private individuals also. Apart from these, many other state owned companies, which are incurring losses, are being transferred but not those industries, which yield high revenue to the government. In fact the government witnessed to transfer the companies, which incur losses and expected high budget assistance from the government to run. So, it is the dualistic system of privatization in Nepal.

Nepal's Privatization: A Dilemma

Successful privatization in any country requires bold decisions and encourage private sector. Privatization depends on the government. (The policy to be taken by the government is an integral part of privatization). So, privatization should be reviewed not as an end in itself but as one of many means to help government interested in fostering a new decision of economic and social activities between the public and private sector. By encouraging private sector, the aim of the economic goals, stated in the periodic plans can be achieved through mobilizing the scattered resources of the individuals. But to mobilize the resources in underdeveloped countries like ours is different due to the fact that the government of Nepal has adopted a trial and error method in formulating the policy decision. As a consequence, the policy and legal environments have not been conducive to foster entrepreneurial behaviour. So, business confidence may be lacking, compliance with the law may be low and small market size severely limits domestic competition.

As mentioned above the capital formation is low on the one hand and entrepreneurial capacity of the people is inadequate on the other. In this regard, masses of people have little knowledge of their potential resources. They have little knowhow about their development possibilities and excess to the outside world. Therefore, they are away from the main stream of national development. Privatization in a country like Nepal hinders the nationals because they do not have adequate capital and sufficient knowledge to run the business. Nepal is looking for entrepreneurial capacity and people who have such type of capacity do not want to bear the risk and uncertainty. In such a situation they would prefer to have their capital either in the form of bank deposit or invest in trading business. Nepal's present position has been characterized by the profit earning business because people who have share in the companies are not active due to the fact that the management of such companies remains with the government. The private communities or individuals are not directly involved in managing the organization. As a result of this, they are only concerned with the dividend. Hence privatization in Nepal is fully dependendent upon foreign capital, foreigners and foreigner's entrepreneurial capacity. The foreigners will operate such companies only, which yield maximum benefit to them. They will not be interested in any productive line of production, which fulfills the basic needs of the people if it has less profit prospects. So, the government should formulate a conducive policy to promote the national joint venture enterprise by giving technical assistance and necessary capital support.

Conclusion

Nepal's initiation in privatizing the economic activities has bitter experience. Though trade, education and forestry are the resulting main sectors and are sought to be privatized fully or partially, they have not been privatized satisfactorily. People are not well-prepared to take up the proposed economic burden by mobilizing their own resources, when previously the government undertook it.

In case of company shares, it is difficult to find adequate capital because almost all the developing countries of the world are characterized by the dearth of capital formation. Hence, it is beyond the reach of the people to buy such shares. In such a situation the foreigners can be encouraged to invest in the shares of the companies. But this will involve an outflow of capital from the country in the form of dividend, profit and services. It is necessary, therefore that the policy of privatization must be thought and right strategy should be adopted.

4.2 PROPERTY TAX: SOME BASIC ISSUES AND PROBLEMS IN UDC'S*

Introduction

A tax is a levy, which a government imposes on its citizens with a view of collecting and mobilizing adequate resources for the development of the economy. There are various forms of taxes, which could be formulated and imposed directly or indirectly. Generally, pattern, structure and the government with its fiscal policies enacts composition of taxation. The income-tax, land-tax and land registration fee etc. all categorized under direct taxation whereas commodity tax, custom duties, production tax etc. are categorized under the indirect taxation. Many forms of taxation, whether they are direct or indirect are introduced together with the fiscal policy for a year to come. In under-developed countries, the main source of the government revenue comes through the land tax. However, some part of the government revenue is composed by the import-export duties and direct taxes.

The following table presents the Percentage of Tax revenue of South Asian countries (1989)

* Published in RAJASWA Year 12, Vol. 2, 1993, pp. 35-42.

TABLE 4.1
Percentage of Tax Revenue

Country	*Taxes on income, profit and capital gains*	*Domestic taxes on goods & services*	*Taxes on international trade and transactions*	*Other taxes*	*Total current revenue if a % of GNP.*
Bangladesh	11.7	33.2	31.5	7.1	8.8
Nepal	20.8	8.6	46.2	12.7	6.2
India	13.5	35.5	26.7	0.4	15.4
Pakistan	10.8	33.4	32.9	0.2	17.8
Sir Lanka	11.0	48.1	28.5	4.1	21.6

Source: World Development Report (1991)

It is obvious from the above table that Nepal has a least percentage of tax composition from domestic taxes on goods and services due to insignificant productive sector of Nepalese economy. So, public sector could play a vital role for the mobilization of the resources through various forms of taxation to gear up the public investment in the production sector of the economy. The inherent responsible factor in such an economy is that the private sector is not conducive to invest its resources in the productive sector is to be channelized by the government itself. In such a situation, an individual or a family or a group of person own assets in the form of cash, kind, transferable asset from one person to another, bank account and investment of the taxpayer. The tax property refers all kinds of fixed and a variable asset i.e. if the government (through its fiscal policy) imposes tax on individual's assets, which is owned in any form, is called the property tax.

Property tax In Nepal

After the restoration of multi-party system HMG/N has tried to introduce the property tax in Nepal. Though this concept was introduced in 1960 A.D. too, but it is still a new concept for successful implementation. Property tax is a tax which is imposed on the nationals according to the evaluation of their holding property with them. Since 1990 the government has introduced property tax in Nepal with the primary exemption of two millions. In Nepal 9 per cent of the total population gets its livelihood in few developed urban centers whereas 91 per cent of the total population resides in the rural area of the country. The rural people are inherited with absolute poverty. Their livelihood depends upon subsistence agriculture farming. So, they are characterized under very low level of income. But the situation seems just opposite in urban centers of Nepal. By virtue of development and employment opportunities people can earn more from various sources. The urban centers are characterized by the facilities of education, health, employment opportunities, which are responsible factors for the people to remain in urban centers. So, the Government of Nepal has introduced property tax in few selected urban centers of the country. The revenue estimated to be collected was Rs. 2.5 crore from property tax in the fiscal year 1992/93 A.D.

Justification of Property Tax in Nepal

Because of spontaneous growth of urban centers in Nepal a vast bulk of wealth is concentrated in these centers throughout the country. Wealthier people of the country are diversifying their resources from rural to urban areas. Such resources are continuing to be invested on real estate. An interrupted flow of resources into real estate and luxury housing would not be conducive for the promotion of high rate of growth. The economy needs a greater volume of investment in the productive sector. But the available resources of the country are directed towards investment in real estate. An investment in real estate tends to generate a large multiplier effect, which enables to accelerate the inflationary situation in the economy. In other words, the investment on large available resources in real estate tends to create high inflation in the economy. In this context, a tax on property seems highly essential to mobilize the resources in under-developed countries like Nepal. For the acceleration of continuous high and stable economic growth, the development of the productive sector is an essential factor.

In this connection the property tax has numerous potentialities of resource mobilization in Nepal. The process of economic development tends to be accompanied by a boom in real estate and an investment in luxury housing and other forms of assets, which do not contribute, to the production of essential commodities in the urban areas. So, in this respect, the concept of property tax is justifiable to mobilize the unproductive resources towards productive sector. Thus the policy of imposing tax on property helps to establish the real sector of an economy, which could create more employment to the unemployed resources on the one hand and discourage to the nationals to invest their resources in real estate and other forms of asset on the other. But, so far as the implementation of property tax in Nepal is concerned, Nepal is still not experienced in this area. Therefore, many cautious actions should be taken into consideration by the government itself when the property taxes have to be implemented.

Evaluation of the Distribution of Ownership of Property

Once however the ownership of property is emphasized as an important factor determining distribution of income, it becomes essential to investigate the variations of amount of property owned. The property owned by an individual at a point of time could be divided into two components. Original property presumably inherited property and own property, which he has accumulated himself. For instance, an individual with inherited property of k_0 at the beginning of the period t_1 will have at the beginning of the period t_n, total property k_{n-1} which could be decomposed into inherited property and accumulated property in two alternative ways is as follows:

(a) $K_{n-1} = K_0 + S(1 + sr)^{n-2}(E_1 + rko) + S(1+sr)^{n-3}(CE_2 + rko) + \ldots\ldots\ldots S(E_{n-1} + rko).$

(b) $K_{n-1} = K_0(1+sr)^{n-1} + (1+sr)^{n-2}E_1 + S(1+sr)n^{-2}E_1 + S(1=sr) + SE_{n-1}.$

where,

$E_1, E_2 \ldots E_{n-1}$ is income from work in period $t_1, t_2 \ldots t_{n-1}$ respectively.

S = is the proportion of income saved, independent of composition of total income and assumed to be same in each period,

r = is the rate of return in property, again assumed to be the same in each period.

The first alternative in effect treats inherited property as datum and regard property accumulated from both earnings and from return from original property as own property. The second treats property accumulated from earnings only as own property. If an individual do not inherit any property (i.e. k_o =o) his total property at the beginning of the period t_n is a function of his earnings in successive periods, his saving propensity and rate of return on property. The above-mentioned model will help to find out the distribution of income in a given society, which forms the basis of evaluating the property for tax base.

Some Basic Actions

If the governments of under-developed countries (UDC's) are ambitious to collect and mobilize the resources collected through its nationals, the governments should ask themselves about how to whom and where to tax. For the answers of these questions, following are some factors that must be evaluated prior to introducing the property tax.

In the first place, a suitable base of the tax has to be determined. In this context, the government should have adequate reasons, which could establish the basis for the property tax. One important reason of mobilizing resources from unproductive sector to productive one. Similarly, the policy of the property tax should also be clear whether the tax is to be levied on the annual rental value of the property or on its capital value.

In the second place, an equitable and accurate valuation is essential. This is the most important and crucial issue with respect to the property tax in almost all under-developed countries. For highly developed countries the development of computerized database has made it possible to evaluate the property of an individual systematically. But in under-developed countries due to lack of highly mechanized system it is difficult to evaluate the value of an individual property. So in this respect an effective and unbiased revenue administration is essential. Because the individual property valuation depends upon the revenue administration, biased and unjustifiable revenue administration could not and will never evaluate the property of individuals fairly and equitably. In such a situation, an effective and reasonable valuation of property is impossible. So, the government policies towards the property taxation should also be clear and it should also take attention to formulate the unbiased and fair revenue administration to an effective and successful implementation of taxation in our country. Therefore, the government should take due attention to the revenue administration to be fair and equitable for the evaluation of property for an individual.

In the *third* place, a suitable structure of tax base has to be determined.

Basic Problems

There are various problems for the implementation of successful property taxation. In under-developed countries like ours,

Firstly, the governments efficiency and its independence from the political pressure are far from expectation. So, to implement and evaluate the property taxation the government should have an independent authority, free from political pressure, and government should follow the policy of recognizing other existing political parties to formulate the policies of property taxation. But in our country the past experience shows that the government is not free to choose alternatives from the party politics and government fails to recognize and respect the creative and productive works of all opposition parties.

Secondly, as stated above, the administrative efficiency is more important when evaluating the property of an individual without taking any substantial base and to implement the property tax policy in the country. But the administrative efficiency is directly related with the government efficiency. In other words, administrative efficiency is a function of government efficiency, or the administrative efficiency is solely dependent on the existing government efficiency. So, government should itself be fair and equitable. By making administrative reforms and by increasing the efficiency of revenue administration, the corrupt practices prevailing in the society could be easily wiped out which forms the basis of evaluating the property of am individual fairly and implementing the property taxation properly.

Thirdly, an unequal distribution of property within a community requires a progressive and proportional tax system, so that one would pay the property tax according to the volume of property owned.

Lastly, In under-developed countries, the character of the people is also under-developed. It is due to the fact that people are uneducated, irresponsive and ignorant about the tax why it is levied. So, other dubious factors may appear both from the point of view of the administrative staff and tax-payer as well.

Thus, it requires fair and equitable property tax. Otherwise corruption will increase which is responsible for evading the revenue from property tax in substantial amount, that would increase the expenditure of the government without collecting the revenue from it. Therefore, a welfare government should take due attention to check the corrupt practices when implementing the property taxation in the country.

Policies for Correcting Tax Evasion

Once the government imposes property tax on its citizens in the urban areas of the country, the government would not be able to check the tax evasion unless and until the government does not workout proper policies for correcting tax evasion. It is a great challenge in under-developed economy because the system of checking the tax evasion has not yet been developed. So, in this respect, the government could formulate a policy to check tax evasion. There are many methods to check tax evasion.

First, the government should follow the policy of distributing telephone line according to the certificate of property tax.

Second, the government should make directions to its financial institutions to distribute the credit in the private sector by taking substantial collateral guarantee together with the tax certificate.

Third, for the nationals who want to visit foreign countries, the government could check the property tax certificate when issuing the visa and passport, and

Lastly, the government could check the tax evasion through the consumption of government provided facilities such as electricity, telephone call, water etc.

Conclusion

The available resources in the country, which are collected through the foreign and domestic sources, and large profit margins in the urban areas is diverted and invested towards real estate and luxury housing in Nepal. As stated above, the investment in such sector creates a boom in the economy. Consumption of luxury goods may increase, as a result of which the economy is pushed into high inflation. So, in this respect, progressive and proportional taxation on property in an equitable and justifiable manner will help discourage the investment in real estate and reduce the consumption of luxury goods as well. Such reduction of investment on unproductive sector of the available resources will tend to diversify into productive sector of an economy. So, the property taxation in under-developed countries, like Nepal, is essential. But the precautions should be taken by the concerned institutions to be fair and equitable when evaluating the property of an individual, and implementing the property taxation for all the citizens who should be taxed.

4.3 CAPTURING THE CRUX OF NEPALESE SOCIETY THROUGH LAND REFORM*

There is an enormous quantity of literature on land tenancy and much of them have treated the questions, how are resources allocated when farmland is used by owner cultivator or alternatively is rented to tenants who pay for it by crop sharing between landlord and tenant? Is land reform aimed at the rent reduction or in transferring land to the tiller? According to one school of thought the stipulation of the crop share lease creates circumstances in which landlord and tenant view their interest separately. Under a crop share lease, if the landlords' share of the crops is half, the tenant will apply his resources in the production of crops until marginal cost of output is equal to half of the value of the marginal output. In the *second* school of thought, landlords are assumed to maximize their rent income subject to constraint of the market wage rate of tenant labour and the agricultural production function. The *third* school of thought, assumed that the removal of dual ownership is desirable in order to increase the land productivity.

Nepal's Experience

The role of the peasantry in the political economy of Nepal since the unification of Nepal until at least the first half of this century, has been to provide the bulk of the surplus on which a ruling aristocracy relied. Over the past four decades, or after the political change in 1951, the then governments one after another have paid attention to implement the land reform programme, but none of the efforts were successful. During the infant stage of Panchayat Autocratic System the Land Reform Act 1964 was enforced, which was an effort to widen the political base of the Panchayat regime. As the consequences, the upper class became beneficiaries from the programme rather than the actual tenants. M.C. Regmi (1976) has rightly remarked that, "'Available evidence indicated that the upper

* Modified from the original paper published in The Economic Journal of Nepal, Vol.18, No 4, 1995, pp.203-07.

rural classes have been the main beneficiaries of the land reforms and the new technology that has been introduced in its wake." Whatever are its outcomes, the land reform programme had threefold primary objectives as follows:

- To uplift and improve general standard of living of those who actually till the land through equitable distribution of holdings.
- To direct and channelize the idle as well as hidden capital and surplus labour from agricultural sector to non-agricultural sector, and
- To increase the economic growth and development in agricultural production.

In order to achieve these goals the Land Reform Act of 1964, had specified a land ceiling of 17 hectare, 4 hectare and 2.5 hectare in the terai, hills and Kathmandu valley respectively. Under this provision the government acquired only meager land 1.2 per cent of total cultivated land. Under the tenancy rights, the tenants were made legally eligible to claim one-fourth share of the product of the land they were tilling. The enforcement of land ceiling was hardly successful. The agricultural census of 1961 and 1971 showed that the percentage of families holding more than 2.68 hectare and owning more than 45 per cent of the land dropped slightly from 7.9 to 6.4 and families holding less than 0.4 hectare rose form 49 per cent to 55 per cent. However, the tenancy right of the tiller guaranteed by the Act is in operation activity.

The main reasons, among other things, of the unsuccessful implementation of land reform programmes were:

- domination of the upper rulings class
- lack of cadastral survey and data base;
- vague definition of individual or family;
- lack of honest and efficient administration;
- lack of bold commitment of the government; and
- lack of people consciousness etc.

Restoration of Multi-party Democratic System and Land Reform

Many thinkers, politicians and economists find themselves

that the productivity of land will increase if the removal of dual ownership is implemented. Most of the land in Nepal is owned by non-tiller and the actual tiller is not the master of land. The Agricultural Sample Census of 1991 shows that more than 50 per cent farming families posses less than a hectare of land and their economic condition is considerably poor. Therefore, in order to increase the agricultural production, a system of equitable distribution of productive resources and the production is required. After the restoration of multiparty democratic system in 1990, the first elected government formulated the Eighth Five Year Plan (1992-97), which explicitly mentions the land reform programme to be made effective. The Eight-Five Year Plan has set the following objectives with regard to land reform and management:

- To discourage the tendency of holding excessive land in agriculture and direct the investment to non-agricultural sector;
- To achieve increase in production and productivity through equitable distribution of land; and
- To update map and land ownership data regularly by determining actual land areas.

In order to achieve these objectives the policies of the plan envisaged to abolish duel ownership to treat Guthi land tenancy rights at par. But the NC government in its three and a half years of tenure could not play an effective role to formulate a land reform programme and its implementation. Although, the government of UML came into office after the mid-term election at the end of 1994 and in campaign, pledged to enforce the land reforms in order to abolish the dual ownership of land by fixing reasonable land ceiling based on the topographical structure of the country, but it could not bring any concrete programmes and policies in its annual budget. Similarly, the present coalition government has also committed to implement the land reform programme without any specific policy action.

Present State of Affair of Land Holdings

According to the Agricultural Census 1991, there are an estimated 2,74 million agricultural holdings in Nepal. The number of agricultural holdings has grown steadily over the last 30 years. In the first Agricultural Census 1961 there were 1,54 million agricultural holdings in the country, 1,20 million less than in 1991.

TABLE 4.2
Size of Land Holdings

Size of the holding	*Holding Number*	*Area of holding*
< 1 hectare	69.5	30.5
1-2 hectare	19.6	27.6
2-3 hectare	6.2	15.4
3-4 hectare	2.2	7.8
4-5 hectare	1.1	4.8
5-10 hectare	1.2	8.1
> 10 hectare	0.3	5.8

Source: National Sample Census of Agriculture, Nepal 1991/92, NPC/CBS/HMG, 1994.

The above figures reveal that 69.5 per cent of landholder's hold only 30.5 per cent of the total cultivated land. The size of the holding of land of the majority of people is only less than one hectare. But 19.6 per cent of the population holds 27.6 per cent of total cultivated land with the size of land holding 1-2 hectare and 0.3 per cent of the landholders has occupied the 5.8 per cent of total cultivated land.

Inequality in the Distribution of Land

The inequality in the distribution of land is analyzed with the help of Gini Coefficient. Higher the value of G i.e nearer to 1 less equitable in the distribution of land because the value of G lies between 0 and 1.

TABLE 4.3
Value of Gini Coefficient in Different Agricultural Census of Nepal

Year	*Value of G*
1961	0.64
1971	0.63
1981	0.65
1991	0.52

Source: Compiled by the Author on the Basis of National Sample Census of Agriculture, Nepal 1991/92, NPC/CBS/HMG, 1994.

From the above figures, it is found that the Gini Coefficient for Nepal as a whole declined between 1961 and 1971 from 0.64 to 0.63. The equality in land distribution has been reduced by 0.01 in 1971 compared to 1961. But the inequality in the distribution of land has increased in 1981, showing that there is a greater inequality as compared to 1961 and 1971. The Gini Coefficient of 1991 comes to 0.52, which signifies that the land distribution is more equitable compared to 1961, 1971 and 1981. This value is enough to draw the inferences that the land distribution in Nepal is extremely unequal. Similarly, in the Agricultural Census of 1991 the Gini Coefficients were 0.54, 0.43 and 0.45 in terai, hill and mountain respectively, showing there is higher inequality in the distribution of land in terai region compared with that of hill and the mountain regions. Likewise the Gini Coefficient is 0.52, 0.49, 0.51 and 0.54 in eastern, central, western, mid-western and far-western development regions respectively.

Conclusion

Virtually, Nepal is a poor country with agrarian based economy. During the past decades the per capita income of Nepal ranges from US $ 160 to US$180. Majority of its people are poor having less than 0.40 hectare of land. Under such perspective, excessive concentration of land in a few hands results in growing landless class. So, equitable land distribution and occupancy rights should be given to the tenants who actually till the land. The experiences show that the reasonable land ceiling will allow a real margin in redistributing the land. The reform programme must be introduced immediately so that vicious circle poverty is not widened. Many empirical studies show that the increase of poverty in Nepal lies in the rural area, yet within the duration of four and half decades, no effective land reform programme is commenced, whether there is a political change or not.

4.4 OPERATING VAT IN THE PRESENT

Many developing countries of the world have been experiencing VAT since late 1960's. They have collected a considerable amount of revenue through VAT. Nepal has also been trying to implement the VAT system. But some controversial issues are being raised because of objections. These objections are based on the argument that comprehensive preparation is needed before VAT is enforced.

This article focuses on defining VAT and its consequences on consumers and producers. VAT is a general multistage tax. Except for some items, which are zero-rated and some exempt items, all goods and services are subject to VAT. It is multistage as it is collected as the proportion of value added at every stage of the production process. VAT disguises its real effects, as it is multistage. The final effect of VAT is the same as the effect of the single stage sales tax at the retail level. It is a straight forward tax on consumers.

VAT is an alternative means of tax collection. VAT replaces the purchase or sales tax at the retail level for the same purpose. It has several stages in which the tax is imposed on goods and services. It takes into account intermediate goods as well as services under taxation before the final goods are produced and sold in the market. VAT is the newest form of commodity taxation. Usually considered and employed as a form of sales tax, it was started from early 1950 but its application was started in 60s.

France and West Germany were the originators of this application. The UK also introduced VAT in 1973 as a qualification to enter into the EEC. Upto 1973, the rate of VAT was fixed as 10 per cent but it has varied.

To understand VAT in a simple manner, one should know the production process. Let us take a case of the shoe production process. Consider all types of raw materials except those of investment goods because VAT is subject to consumer's goods not for investor's goods. When a consumer buys shoes it has been through several stages of production. A pair of shoes would have started off as raw leather, thread, needle, polish etc. Each subsequent process is subject to VAT.

TABLE 4.4
Procedure for Value Added Tax

Stage of production	*Total value of goods*	*Value added at each stage*	*VAT 15%*
Raw leather	60.00	60.00	9.00
Tanning process	130.00	70.00	10.50
Cutting and Sizing	210.00	80.00	12.00
Sewing and Polishing	300.00	90.00	13.50
Services	400.00	100.00	15.00
Total		400.00	60.00

Retail Price + VAT = 400 + 60 = 460

The value added at each stage of production is equal to the difference between the value of input and the value of output. The stages of production are shown in the table above (4.4) in order to make it easier to understand how VAT operates in each of production process. Finally, the same amount is levied from VAT as the single stage sales tax in retail prices. The distinguishing feature of VAT when separated from sales tax is that it includes all types of services incurred during the production process of final goods.

Production is free from the tax burden. They only have the administrative burden of tax collection and record keeping. As stated above, any machinery or depreciation of machinery is not liable to VAT, which is a tax on consumption not on investment.

But things are not so simple as discussed. The situation will be favourable to producers, if people have choices between taxed and untaxed goods or between taxed spending and untaxed saving, then their behaviour will change. This happens not through consciousness but because the higher prices of taxed goods lead people to buy less. This will no doubt have an effect on manufacturers and employees.

Shifting the burden of VAT on to producers will certainly affect prices; lower the output, lower profits, lowers jobs in the economy. In designing a VAT system for developing countries like Nepal, the following policies should be adopted:

- VAT should be extended to include retail tax.
- Very small firms should not be included in the VAT regime and the primary sector should be excluded.
- All services excepting health care and education should be brought under VAT.
- A uniform levy should be imposed but a differentiated rate is desirable for those goods and services, which are most essential for the people in general.
- The design of confessional rate of VAT will be suitable for avoiding the differentiated rate of VAT.
- A basket should be made for goods for zero rating.
- A policy of tax exemption for necessary goods should be designed.

Being simple in nature, VAT is a complex tax. It would however be an important mechanism if co-ordination were brought about between domestic and foreign trade taxes. The relevant experience with VAT is that it can be implemented in low income countries successfully for the reason that there are some advantages in collecting a more sizable revenue through VAT than from lump-sum sales tax system.

4.5 FOREIGN AID: A CURSE IN DISGUISE

Development efforts in Nepal started only after the initiation of the first Five-Year Plan in 1956. But prior to this period also, adhoc development works were commenced after the downfall of the Rana regime in 1951. Nepal has completed seven five-year plans, each with its own attractive targets, objectives and policies. Currently, the country is nearing the end of the 8th five-year plan (1992-97).

However, the successive plans cannot be said to have made any remarkable achievement in realizing their objectives and uplifting the economic and social well being of the people. Development reports show that the country is not only poor on the economic front but also one of the lowest in the human development index.

This is mainly because the policies of successive governments could not adequately mobilize the domestic resources. As a result, the heavy dependence on foreign resources led the country and the people to bear a heavy debt burden. The three consecutive decades, 1950's, 1960's and 1970's to some extent, were most fruitful for Nepal's development in mobilizing the external sources.

Most of the infrastructure development work like roads, electricity, industries, irrigation, health facilities, etc., took place in the same period. Inspite of the development of these facilities with the help of foreign resources, the well-being of the country and its people leaves much to be desired for. The per capita income of the people could not exceed US$ 180. The growth rate of GDP scarcely equals the population growth rate and more than 60 per cent of the people live below the poverty line.

After the restoration of multi-party democracy in Nepal, the annual growth rate of foreign loan has been 24 per cent. Prior to the year 1990, Nepal had Rs.36.8billion foreign loan outstanding. The foreign loan outstanding after the restoration of multi-party system in Nepal is given in table 4.5.

From the table 4.5 it is obvious that the foreign loan reached 121.4 billion after the change in the political system of Nepal in 1990. During this period of six years, Nepal has received three times the foreign loan outstanding up to 1989/90. An unhealthy aspect of this increase in foreign loan is the steady decline in the development of economic and social services. Therefore, Nepal has not been too optimistic about economic and social services development, and no remarkable

TABLE 4.5
Fiscal Year Foreign Loan Outstanding

(Rs. in billion)

up to	1989/90	36.8
"	1990/91	59.5
"	1991/92	70.9
"	1992/93	87.4
"	1993/94	102
"	1994/95	113
"	1995/96	121.4*

Source: Economic Survey, FY 1995/96, MOF/HMG* includes first nine months.

development work has taken place during the same period of time.

The foreign aid over the three decades had been utilized through direct approach of the donor agencies. But at present, especially after the restoration of multi-party democracy in Nepal, there has been an expansion of foreign loan (from Rs. 36.9 billion to Rs. 121.4 billion) – separate from the foreign grants –for the development of the economy. In this context, Nepali policy makers have become passionately fond of anything foreign. This foreign phobia has become so widespread today that there is no sector of area that is free from foreign influence. As a result, the Nepali economy has now become subservient to its foreign friends.

As previously stated, during the six-year period, the foreign loan increased at the rate of 24 per cent per annum. However, the overall performance of the economy shows a declining trend. This is proved by the human development report of 1996 published by the United Nations Development Program (UNDP) where Nepal is placed in the 151st position out of 174 countries of the world. This is due to the lack of wholehearted commitment for the development of the economy. There is a narrow focus on development perspective, which is mainly based on the subjective criteria with short-term vision.

It is obvious that the decision makers have a narrow view on the long-term development perspective due to the fact that they are motivated by the short-term undue advantage of political games.

Nepal is among the poorest countries of the world. Over the past six years various programs of rural development and poverty alleviation have been set up for the sake of obtaining foreign loan and grant.

This huge amount of foreign loan has brought the evil consequence of inflation in the economy due to lack of farsightedness of the decision makers to consolidate this resource into the productive sectors of the economy.

Thus, we have a loan outstanding of Rs. 121.4 billion with no marked improvement in the living standard of the people. The programs and policies are set only for getting the loan from external sources and they do not benefit those for whom they are intended and implemented. In direct contrast, the corrupt in the society benefit as is seen from the recent policy of the government to increase the allowance and salary of ministers and parliamentarians.

4.6 CAN PRIVATIZATION BE SUCCESSFUL?

The transfer of economic activities of a country from the public sector to private sector is called privatization. In other words privatization means less control and regulation by the state in economic activities. Or, it is the denationalization, liberalization and deregulation of the economic activities by the state.

Since 1980's the government of Nepal has made attempts to privatize the state owned companies by selling ownership of the state to the private sector. But the successive governments have been unsuccessful in privatizing the state owned enterprises except for a few companies in the field of social services.

After the restoration of multi-party system in 1990, the first elected government of Nepali Congress Party, during its three and half years of tenure had followed the policy of privatizing state owned enterprises as one of the major thrusts of the economic reform.

As a consequence, some of the major state owned enterprises of the country such as Bansbari Leather and Shoe Company, Harishidhi Bricks & Tile Company and Bhrikuti Paper & Pulp Industry has already been transferred to the private sector during the same period of time.

The then major political parties of the country were not in consensus about the process of privatization followed by the Nepali Congress. This momentum of privatization was adjourned when the government of CPN (UML) came to office at the end of 1994.

After the formation of the coalition government, some ten months ago brisk efforts are made to continue the same process of privatization, which was started during the period of the Nepali Congress government two years ago.

Regarding the transfer of state owned enterprises to private sector, there are differences of opinion in the public minds like:

(a) The transfer of ownership of the state to private sector of the enterprises may warm the hearts of investment bankers, consultants, lawyers, domestic as well as foreign investors and workers of the enterprises to be privatized.

(b) Unemployment situation may be created due to the rapid change in the working style of the new management.

(c) The fraudulent pricing of the goods and services lead the society to be suspicious of the motive of the investors.

This is especially the case in the society like ours where the public confidence in the government is low, and corruption is perceived as a normal part of the administrative and political process.

At present, the coalition government is in the process of privatizing Telecommunication Corporation but the public opinion is divided. Even the parliament is not unanimous in the same for the above-mentioned reasons. The largest political party of the country the CPN (UML) has already expressed its views against privatization of Telecommunication Corporation.

There is also mixed opinion among the member parties of the coalition government. The major parties of Nepal are still in confusion and feel that it is difficult to find adequate capital because Nepal is characterized by the dearth of the capital formation.

Therefore, it is beyond the reach of the people to buy such shares. In such a situation, foreigners can be encouraged to invest in the shares of the corporation. But this process of privatization will involve an outflow of capital from the country in the form of dividend, profit and services.

The experience show that the process of privatization in Nepal has not yet been able to get maturity due to the dearth of capital in public hands. The transfer of two companies during the period of 1990-94 was the example of selling the ownership to the foreigners.

As mentioned above, it is unfortunate to say that people doubt the integrity of the financial institutions and officials who manage the privatization process and carry out the evaluation and transfer of state ownership of the enterprise to be privatized.

Another reason for unsuccessful privatization is the state of letter confusion about entrepreneurial capacity of the people, inadequate capital and in sufficient knowledge to run the business. Therefore, privatization in Nepal, in the present context is fully dependent upon the foreign capital and foreign entrepreneurial capacity.

In this context, it can be concluded that public sentiment about privatization varies from critical acceptance to outright protest. People feel it is difficult to rely on government to make objectives appraisal of property value on the one hand and the public has an interest in every company that is to be privatized on the other.

It is prepared to question the rationale behind every decision regarding the sale of public property, particularly when the buyer is a foreigner. The major political party CPN

(UML) has protested the process of privatization in the parliament as well as in the street. Amid such confusion the privatization question should be first resolved by the parliament in the interest of the nation and her people.

4.7 RESOURCE MOBILIZATION AND TAXATION

One of the fundamental issues of resource mobilization and development in Nepal relates to the existence of widespread and persistent poverty. An absolute poverty is overwhelmingly concentrated in rural areas although significant proportion of the urban population also fails to get its basic needs met.

Nepal is a poor country having a per capita income of less than US $ 180. There is still a large subsistence sector due to the very low level of economic development. Prior to the Fiscal Year 1995/96, Nepal had no annual budget, although the revenue of the government was collected through land and income taxes.

But for the first time in Nepal's economic history the government prepared and presented a budget to the people in 1952/53. Observing the revenue structure of that period, one finds it typically that of a traditional economy with 73 per cent of the government revenue coming from non-tax sources and land tax. The share of the non-tax sources alone was 43 per cent.

Tax revenue is usually considered under two headings: direct and indirect taxes. Direct taxes include taxes on personal and corporate income, taxes on wealth and property as well as land tax etc. Similarly, indirect taxes are levied in specific goods on international trade.

In Nepalese tax structure, the indirect tax has contributed the predominant share of the total tax revenue. The structure of Nepalese tax revenue for 1989/90–1993/94 period is presented in terms of direct and indirect tax revenue.

For the convenience of calculation, the indirect taxes are classified in two broad categories; (a) customs, and (b) tax on consumption of products, goods and services. The contribution of indirect taxes on the average is 82.3 per cent during the five-year period. This is because of heavy dependence on foreign imports due to the low level of industrialization and large exports of primary products. The major revenue of the government is collected from the commodity taxes. During the same period, the tax on consumption and production of goods and services remains highest, nearly about 47 per cent of the total tax revenue of the government followed by 35 per cent of the total tax revenue from customs. The annual growth rate of indirect taxes during the same period is 19 per cent followed by 16.8 and 20.8 per cent in the annual growth of customs and tax on consumption, goods and services respectively.

Similarly, the direct taxes are divided into two broad categories: (a) Land revenue and registration, and (b) Tax on profit, property and income. As stated above, poverty in Nepal is associated with low level of income, low growth of national production, poor employment opportunities and degenerating economic base as land becomes increasingly scarce and unproductive and labour force is unable to meet the consumption demands.

The exemption limit and the proportion of people subject to income tax also vary. Consequently, the share of direct taxes to the total tax revenue is 17.7 per cent during the same period, and the non-tax revenue contributed 24 per cent share to total revenue. The tax revenue has a declining trend with an annual growth rate of 18.5 per cent.

Tax structure does not seem to have served the other possible objectives of facilitating efficiency in social distribution. It is purely due to the tax structure that trade and commerce of a speculative nature has become the most attractive economic activity in the private sector. According to the analysis made in a study of IDS, residential construction and real estate development are perceived to be the most lucrative form of investment with the output of these sectors showing the highest growth rate among all the sectors contributing to the country's GDP.

Nepal's tax revenue is dependent mainly on accruals from taxes on international trade and goods and services supplemented from taxes on income and property to some extent. A major feature of the tax structure is the heavy dependence on taxes, which constituted more than 82.3 per cent of the total tax revenue within the time span of 1989/90 – 1993/94.

The above analysis reflects the poor mobilization of internal resources. The percentage of tax revenue to GDP remains almost constant in the first four years and this percentage was increased by one per cent in 1993/94.

Therefore, in order to reduce the deficit of the government finance and to achieve the accelerated rate of growth of the economy, a new capital formation should be created. The structural reform of the existing tax on a broad base and to make the current taxation more effective is also essential.

4.8 THE BUDGET OF FY 1993/94: A CHALLENGE TO DEMOCRATIC SOCIALISM

While over 60 per cent of the population is facing absolute poverty, low level of income and subsistence living has added more to their plight. The per capita income from the past decades remain between US$160 and 170. The population is increasing at the annual growth rate of 2.08. The growth rate of GDP is only about 2.9 per cent. Amid such an economic scenario the government has claimed that substantial achievement is made in the economic front in the past two years. Accordingly, the Finance Minister has presented a proposed budget expenditure of 35513.9 million rupees for the fiscal year 1993/94. The proposed budget seems to be no better than a duplication of previous year's budget with an increase in expenditure of about 5.7 per cent. Out of the total budget, 22625.9 million rupees comprise the development expenditure and 12888.0 million rupees constitute regular expenses. The revenue sources of the budget is expected to be raised from different sources, as given below:

TABLE 4.6
Proposed Revenue of the FY 1993/94

Sources	*Revenue in %*
Internal sources	46.24
External sources	43.95
Budget deficit	9.81

The above figures show that the budget expenditure is dominated by foreign loan and grants. Against this backdrop one can only say that the internal resources would be enough only to meet administrative expenses on the one hand and repayment of interest on the other. Hence, one can safely predict that the infrastructure and volume of investment that the economy demands to expand its capital formation will virtually be dependent on the foreign sources. Without adequately developing infrastructure by mobilizing resources of our own, it is not only difficult but also equally impossible to find adequate resources from the foreign sources.

Similarly 9.81 per cent budget deficit can be taken as the excess amount of the proposed budget of the fiscal year 1993/94. If the proposed amount is diverted towards the real productive sector; the economy will run smoothly. If the amount is directed to the unproductive sector of a economy, it will have devastating consequences. It will certainly raise the money supply, which will be one of the major causes of high inflation. It will also equally increase the high internal debt. One of the serious challenges faced by the Nepalese economy lies in the fact that the investment of private sector is not channelized to the real and productive sector. The budget remains a silent witness towards the sound policy of diverting funds from the unproductive to productive one.

From the viewpoint of overall perspective of the budget some of the remarkable features can be listed as

(1) the maintenance of stability in the overall sphere,

(2) liberalization, and

(3) sustainable rural development through decentralization.

Reviewing these features one can safely say that the

political instability caused by the political parties from the beginning stands as one of the major problems. Against such scenario existing, the proposed budget may certainly fail to achieve its economic objectives.

For the fulfillment of its economic goal, the budget has sought the privatization and liberalization of the economy. But it fails to give proper policy direction and needed incentives to the private investors except lowering the interest rate. Neither the budget is fully directed towards the open market system nor it catches the norm of the mixed and socialistic economic system on the whole. So the proposed budget seems to be a dubious runner without a broad horizon.

Hence, the proposed budget is traditional and seriously lacks the force to meet challenges faced by the Nepalese economy. The fact is that the majority of the people of Nepal are below poverty line but there is no poverty alleviation programme mentioned in the budget. Similarly, due to the high internal debt and money circulation it is almost impossible for the government to achieve its goal of economic stabilization, economic reforms and rural development.

The budget has claimed that by adopting the concept of privatization and liberalization, it has invited entrepreneurs for a number of tourism based and agro-based industries. Similarly, by liberalizing and decentralizing the economy, the government has claimed that the foreign investors are attracted to invest in the country. But lack of infrastructure and political stability, the government has a bleak chance to achieve this goal. Electricity problem has adversely affected the possibilities of foreign investment. The gross power generation at present has not been able to meet the additional national demand of 30 MW annually in the country.

The budget has also claimed that the average rate of inflation has dropped down to a single digit. It envisages that the current rate of inflation, during the fiscal year 1993/94, will remain between 5 and 6 per cent. The average inflation rate however comes down not because of increase in internal production but because of the evaluation of Nepalese currency against Indian currency. So that the imported goods and services from India become cheaper as compared to the goods and services imported from the third countries. But the inflation rate is increasing with respect to domestic goods and services. The prices of essential commodities such as milk, sugar, electricity, telephone, kerosene, meat, rice, ghee, fertilizer. etc are on the rise. With this price hike in essential commodities the fixed income group of people are affected significantly. No remarkable measures have been taken to control the price rise in such consumers' items. Therefore, the proposed budget is disappointing for the fixed income group, poor and peasants. The budget somehow serves the interest of big businessmen.

The budget proposes to levy one paisa as additional excise duty for a stick of cigarette. It is one of the welcoming steps taken towards discouraging smokers. But the proposed excise duty is unjustifiable for those who smoke low quality brand of cigarettes. Similarly, the budget proposes drastic increase in land revenue. The revenue rates of land seem to be a progressive one but in reality it is a digressive rate of taxation. In fact the land revenue rate should be formulated in accordance to the size of land holding. On the contrary, the budget proposes a flat rate according to the types of land. So the budget is unable to introduce progressive rate of taxation. The budget is directly in favour of big farmers and undermines the poor peasants. Therefore, from the proposed increase in land revenue, small farmers might be affected and it will have negligible effect on big farmers.

4.9 DEVELOPMENT TRAP : NEEDS TO BUILD INSTITUTIONAL BASE

Development in the twentyfirst century will virtually remain a complex phenomenon. The current growth rate of population in the developing countries is sure to bring disaster among the lines of political instability together with the economic hardships. The complexity arises through the development constraint that the governments of developing countries fail to cope with. These countries amid the beginning of 21st century face a development challenge. They find themselves paralyzed in the context of high population growth with increasing deprivation, political instability, low economic growth rate and increasing dependency on developed countries in the development process. Environmental degradation, another problem faced today creates a hardship in the living of the majority of the people. These countries are characterized by the lack of resources to cope with the problems inherited by the degradation of forest as a source of conservation of biodiversity, sanctify power of the agricultural land to keep fertile, amass power of improving degraded environment and wide range of capacity meet the demand of energy. Unfortunately, deforestation is being conducted beyond the capacity of these countries. The revenue of the government is so low, that it cannot be sufficient even to meet the regular expenditure. Borrowing eventually makes up the gap of regular expenditure of the government. In this juncture, the development budget is estimated only at the assertion of the donors.

Majority of the people of thus countries have not even tasted a bit of the fruit of development. Due to expensive health services and education, majority of the people are out of health facilities and education. As a consequence, there is low human development and over 60 per cent of the population is under the capability poor. The livelihood of the majority of the people is the subsistence agriculture and it accounts over 80 per cent of the labour force absorption. The contribution of the industrial sector to the labour force absorption is hardly 10 per cent. In such a perspective, mass unemployment exists and brings a disaster of economic hardship. Creation of new opportunities to offer employment to the growing labour force entails a fair and just commitment, dedication and visionary understanding in the development process in the impartial manner. However, the developing countries have been facing a great crisis of good governance in consonance with the crisis of dedicated leadership.

Nepal is one of the poorest below among the developing

countries with per capita income US $220. Over 80 per cent of the population's livelihood is based on the subsistence agriculture farming. Today this sector absorbs above 80 per cent of the labour force and the labour force remains virtually in the state of under employment. Such factor pushes the unemployed country's youth to go abroad for seeking employment for their livelihood. Visualizing this situation of Nepal, political instability during the last decade dominates the overall scene. As a result of this, low level or even negative economic growth is perceived in the recent years and tends to continue for the years to come.

The economy of Nepal today is in collapsing phase. Some notable basic industries, established in the decades of 1960s and 1970s, do not exist in the condition of operation because of the implemented policy of privatization, deregularization and liberalization. Privatization of the state owned industries is considered to be a right step. However, the implementation policies to privatize the concerned institutions is weak for the reason that most of them have either collapsed or are in the state of liquidation. The process of development needs adequate resources and most of the developing countries of the world, like Nepal are featured by the resource constraint. Mobilization of scarce resources plays a vital role in speeding development on a greater scale. Nepal has poor resource base to undertake the development task on a greater scale. The mobilization of scarce resources is an essential step in undertaking development activities. However, Nepal fails to mobilize scarce resources for the need of minimum requirement for sustainable development and is wholly/ partially depended on the foreign loan/ grant to invest in the development activities.

Development itself cannot take place. It should be based on certain principles. A committed and unselfish leadership as we learn from the history of the developed world is needed to make institutional base strong and impartial, which can monitor and guide the country through the path of development. In this context, impartiality plays a vital role in making institution strong and prosperous. The judgement of the institution should be guided by certain principles that is not influenced or affected by anyone. If unjust judgement, by the head of the institution on the basis of nepotism and favouritism is made then such misdeed brings backward linkages and boosts up the social agitation that might turn up to a devastating result. Such deeds of the institution considered as the pillar of development, push the institution back to the unbelievable situation, lose harmony, incentive, restlessness and discouragement.

During the tenure of twelve years in office, one after the other of the group of national parties of the country, appointed head of the institutions on the basis of the principles of nepotism and favouritism without any notable capacity. This deed pushed the institution into pessimism and finally turned it to a decaying phase. As a result of this people felt bitter because of pessimism and doubted in every action of the institution. Thus, in such a pessimistic environment people devoted themselves in making institution (political, industrial, agricultural, health services, education and many others) fair, just, impartial and strong to drive the country in the optimistic path of development.

Another step in the developing process is building up of institutions that can manage, guide and monitor the action taken in the course of development. To do this, fair, just, honourable and impartial judgement is needed, which may be possible only when the institutional leadership is impartial and capable of itself. However, there is a decaying phase of institutional base in Nepal because of the persistence of three-dimensional political war between king and existing greater parties of the country and the war between rebellious known as Maoists and king and also the war between political parties and Maoists. The situation, now the country is facing, has led the development process in turmoil.

Bibliography

Adhikari C.K. (1990). *"Let us Bank to the Poor"* (Nepali). Human Resources Development Centre, Lalitpur.

Agrawal G. and K.K. Gurugharana (1988). *An Exercise in Macro-econometric Model, Analysis and forecasting, A case Study of US Economy,* Journal of Development and Administration Studies, Vol. 10, No. 1-2, CEDA, T.U. Kirtipur.

Ahman, O.K. *et.al.ed.* (1984). *Converting Water into Wealth,* IIDS, Kathmandu.

American Economic Review (1952). Papers and Proceedings of the 60th Annual Meeting of the American Economic Association,

Ang, B.W. (1988), *Paper Prepared for the APDC/REDP Regional Seminar on sectoral Energy Demand Analysis held at Asian Pacific Development Centre, Kuala Lumpur.*

Asian Development Bank (2000). *Key Indicators of Developing Asian and Pacific Countries,* Vol. XXXI, ADB, 2000.

Baldwin, G.B. (1972). *"A Layman Guides to Little/Mirrless".* Finance and Development Vol. 9, No.

Bangaladesh University of Engineering and Technology, Bangaladesh Academy of Sciences (1985). *International Conference on Energy Development Planning for Bangaladesh,* Dhaka.

Baumol W.J. and M.H. Peston (1955). *More on the Multiplier Effects on the Balanced Budget.* American Economic Review.

Budget Speeches, HMG/N, Ministry of Finance (various issues).

Baumol, W.J. and Wallace Eoats, (1979). *Economics, Environmental Policy and the Quality of Life.* Prentice Hall Inc., Eagle.

Behrman, J.R. (1977). *Macro-economic Policy in a Developing Country,*

The Chilean Experience, North Holland.

Beijer Institute (1997). *Environment and Development Economics, Vol. 2, Part 2,* Cambridge University Press.

B.C. Mehta and G.M.K. Madnani, (1988). Mathematics for Economists, Sixth edition, Sultan Chand and Sons, New Delhi, p. 463.

Bijoness, Inger-Marie, (1992). *Hydro-electric Development in Rural Nepal, A Resource Analysis of Kulekhani Project,* MAB, Kathmandu.

Bluffstone, Randal A., (1998) *Reducing Degradation of Forests in Poor Countries When Permanent Solution Elude Us, What Instruments do we Have?* Environment and Development Economics. *Vol. 3, Part A,* Cambridge University Press.

Butlin, John A., (1981). *Economics and Natural Resources Policy,* Longman, London.

Cassedy, Edward S.,(2000). Prospects for Sustainable Energy, A Critical Assessment, Cambridge University Press.

CBS, (1996)._*Nepal Living Standards Survey Reports.* Vol. I and II, Kathmandu.

CBS, (1998). *A Compendium on Environment Statistics,* CBS/HMG, Kathmandu, Nepal.

CBS, (1995). *Population Monograph of Nepal,* CBS/ HMG, Kathmandu, Nepal.

CBS, (1992, 1996, 2000), *Statistical Pocket Book 1992,* CBS, Kathmandu.

CBS (1991). Census Survey of Agriculture, Kathmandu.

Chishyi, Salim, Nusrat Hasan, and Mahpara Sadaquaet, (1990). *Probability Distribution of Energy Demand Forecasts in Pakistan,* Pakistan Journal of Applied Economics, Vol. IX, No.2.

Dahal, M.K.(1993). *Future of Nepalese Economy,* NEFAS, Kathmandu.

Deshpande, S.A.,(1959). *Labour Surplus and Saving Potential in Underdeveloped Countries,* Indian Economic Journal

Desai, Ashok V. (ed.), (1990). *Energy Economics,* Wiley Eastern Ltd., New Delhi.

.......(1990). *Energy Demand,* Wiley Eastern Ltd., New Delhi.

.......(1990). *Pattern of Energy Use in Developing Countries,* Wiley Eastern Ltd., New Delhi.

Dhungel, K. R. (1992). "A Note on Measures of Inequality and Illustration from Nepalese Health sector", The Economic

Journal of Nepal, Vol. 15, No. 2, CEDECON. T.U, Kirtipur.

Dhungel, K. R. (1999). *Macro Economic in Developing Countries*, Economic Review. Number 11, Nepal Rashtra Bank, Kathmandu.

Dunkerley, J. (1979). *International Energy Strategies*, Cambridge, Massachussets.

ECAFE,(1955). *Economic Development and Planning in Asia and Far East, Problems and Technique*, Economic Bullentin, Vol. VI, No. 3.

Economic Policy for West Asia (1980). *Econometric Planning Model of the Syrian Arab Republic*, Lebanon.

Foell, W.K., J.S.Behring, W.A. Behring, R.L. Dennis, M.E. Hanson, L.A. Hervey, A.Holzl, K.Ito, R.L. Keeney, J.P. Peerenboom, E.Ponitz, J.Richter, A.Toifelhardt, (1981). *The Winconsin-IIASA Set of Energy/Environment (WISE) Models for Regional Planning and Management: An Overview*. International Institute For Applied Systems Analysis, Luxemburg, Austria.

Gamba, Julio R, David A. Caplan and John J. Mulckhayse, (1986). *Industrial Energy Rationalization in Developing Countries*, World Bank, Washington D.C.

Gilbert, A. G and Goodman D.E., (1976), "*Regional Income Disparities and Economic Development, a Critique*" In A.G. Gilbert (ed.) Development Planning and Spatial Structure (London willey)

Gilbert, A. and J. Guglar, (1982) Cities, Poverty and Development. Oxford University Press.

Giovannini, A., (1985). *Saving and Real Interest Rate in LDC's*, Journal of Development Economics, Vol. 18.

Gujarati, D.N.(1995). *Basic Econometrics*, Third Edition, McGraw-Hill Book Co. Singapore.

Gurugharana, K.K. (1992). *Methods of Macro Econometric Modelling in Developing Countries*, The Economic Journal of Nepal, Vol. 15 No. 2, T. U., Kirtipur.

Gurugharana, K.K. (1995) "*Trends and Issue in Poverty Alleviation in Nepal.*" The Economic Journal of Nepal, Vol. 18, No.1, CEDECON. T.U, Kirtipur

Gurugharana, K.K. (1991). "*Poverty Alleviation and Human Development in Nepal, Micro Economic and Sectoral Policies and Programs*". UNDP, Kathmandu

Hall, Charles A.S., Cutler J. Cleveland, Robert Kaufman, (1986). *Energy and Resource Quality: The Ecology of the Economic Process*, John Wiley and Sons, NY.

Hansen, A.H., *Fiscal Policy and Business Cycles*, 1941.

Hansen, Bent, *The Economic Theory of Fiscal Policy*, 1958.

Hansen, J. (1978) *Guidelines to Practical Project Appraisal: Social Benefit Cost Analysis in Developing Countries*, Oxford and IBH Publishing Company, New Delhi.

Haq, Mahbul, ul (1997). *Human Development in South Asia*, Oxford University Press, Karachi.

Haque, Lahiri and P.J. Montiel (1990). *A Macro Econometric Model for Developing Countries*, IMF Staff Paper, Vol. 37, No.3.

Hemming, Richard and Monsoor Ali M., *"Is privatization the Answer"?* Finance and Development, A Quarterly Publication of IMF and World Bank, September 1998, p. 31.

Henkel, R. (1984), *The Distribution of Health Care Services in Zambia With Special Emphasis on the Distribution of the Churches*, Paper presented at the IGU Medical Geograply Conference Lusaka.

Hicks, U.K, *Public Finance*, 1955.

Hill, R, *et.al.* (1995). *The Future of Energy*, Use, Earth Scans Publications Ltd., London.

HMG/ADB (1982) Nepal Agriculture Sector Strategy Study, MOA, HMG, N.

HMG, Ministry of Finance, Budget Speech 1984-85.

Hosier, R.H. and J. Dowd (1987). *Household Fuel in Zimbabwe: An Empirical Test of the Energy Ladder Hypothesis.* Resources and Energy.

IAEE (1997). *Energy and Economic Growth: Is Sustainable Growth Possible*? Vol.I, II, III, IAEE, New Delhi.

ICIMOD, (1986). *Energy For Mountain Districts*,. ICIMOD, Kathmandu.

ICIMOD, (1986). *Energy For Mountain Districts*, ICIMOD, The Economic Journal of Nepal, Vol.12, No. 2, 1989. Kathmandu.

IEA, (1985). *Energy Policy and Programs of IEA Countries*, IEA Paris.

ILO (1977), *Narrowing the Gaps, Planning for Basic Needs and Productive Employment in Zambia*, ILO, Geneva.

Imran, Mudassar and Philip Barnes(1990). *Energy Demand in the Developing Countries: Prospects for Future*, World Bank Staff Commodity Working Paper Number 23, The World Bank, Washington D.C.

Jain, S.C. (1981). *Poverty to Prosperity in Nepal*. Development Publications, Delhi.

James M. Henderson and Richard E. Quandt, *Micro Economic Theory, A Mathematical Approach,* Second edition, McGraw Hill Kogakush Ltd., Tokyo, 1971, p. 374.

Jean Weber, *Mathematical Analysis, Business and Economic Applications,* J.M.C. Press Incorporated, Philippines, 1976, p. 614.

Johonston, J. (1960). *Econometric Methods,* McGraw Hill, N. Y.

Kanel, N.R. (1985). *"Gini Coefficient and Kanel's Reduction, The Economic .... Gini ratio of the Income."* Journal Nepal, Vol. 18, No. (4).

Khanal, D.R. (1990). *Policy Planning Models for the Nepalese Economy With Special Reference to the Industrial Sector,* Unpublished draft Report.

Khatiwada, Yuba Raj, *"The Drive to Privatization in Nepal",* Strategies Study Series, Number 8-10, Center for Nepal and Asian Studies, 1986, p. 74.

Kleindorfer, Paul R. *et al* ed. (1996). *Energy, Environment and Economy, Asian perspectives,* Edward Elgar Publication Ltd. UK.

Klien, L.R. (1971). *Forecasting and Policy Evaluation Using Large Scale Econometric Models,* The State of the Art Frontiers of Quantitative Economics, (ed.), M. D. Strigligator, Amsterdam.

Klien, L.R. and Gold Berger (1955). *An Econometric Model of the US (1929-52),* Amsterdam.

Koo Y. C. Anthony (1973) *"Towards More General Model of Land Tenancy and Reform",* The Quarterly Journal of Economics, Harvard University Press, Cambridge, Massachusetts.

Koutsoyiannis, A. (1977). *Theory of Econometrics,* ELBS, Hongkong.

Kujnets, S. (1995) *"Economic Growth and Income Inequality"* American Economic Review, Vol. 4.

Lahiri, A. (1989). *Dynamics of Asian Savings, The Role of Growth and Age Structure,* IMF Staff Paper, Vol. 36, Washington.

Layard, R. (1974) *Project Appraisal and Planning for Developing Countries,* Oxford and IBH Company, New Delhi.

Layard, R. (1975) (ed.*) Cost Benefit Analysis,* Penguin Books Ltd., England.

Leach, Gerald (1987). *Household Energy in South Asia,* Elsevier Applied Science, London and New York.

Lepton, M. (1983). Poverty Under Nutrition and Hunger. World Bank Staff Working Paper, No. 297, WEB.

Little, I.M.D, Mirrlees, J.A. (1974) *Project Appraisal and Planning for*

Developing Countries, Oxford and IBH Company, New Delhi.

Madala, G.S. (1971). *The Use of Various Component Models in Pooling Cross Section and Time Series Data*, Econometrica, Vol. 39.

Marcus, A.A. (1992). *Controversial Issues in Energy Policy*, Sage Publication, London.

Merlein H.A. and W.C. Harly (1977), Energy Economics, Gulf Publishing Company, Houston, Taxas, USA.

Ministry of Finance (1996). Economic survey FY 1995/96. Kathmandu.

Ministry of Law and Justice, *Nepal Ain Sangraha*, 2047.

Mishan, E.J. (1975) *Cost Benefit Analysis*, George Allen and Unwin.

MOF/HMG, (2001). *Economic Survey*, Kathmandu.

Musgrave, R.A, *Fiscal Policy in Prosperity and Depression.*

Nepal Electricity Authority (2000). *NEA At A Glance*, NEA, Kathmandu.

Nepal Rashtra Bank (1998), A Multiple Household Survey Report, Kathmandu.

NPC (1977). A Survey of Employment, Income and Consumption Pattern in Nepal. HMG/N, Kathmandu.

NPC (1985) The Seventh Plan. HMG/N, NPC, Kathmandu.

NPC (1992). The Eighth Plan. HMG/N, NPC, Kathmandu.

NPC (1992) *Poverty Alleviation and Human Development in Nepal*, Proceedings of National seminars, Kathmandu.

NPC (1997). *An Approach Paper to Ninth Plan*, Kathmandu.

NPC/HMG, The Sixth Plan (2037-42), Kathmandu.

.........(1992). The Eighth Plan (1992-97), Kathmandu

.........(1997), The Approach Paper to Ninth Plan, Kathmandu.

NPC/HMG (1992). *The Eighth Plan*, Kathmandu.

________ (1997). *The Ninth Plan*, Kathmandu.

NPC/UNDO/WB (1992). *Poverty Alleviation and Human Development in Nepal*. Kathmandu.

Parikh, Jyotik (1980). *Energy System and Development*, Oxford University Press, New Delhi.

Pearce, D.W. (1971) *Cost Analysis in Urban and Regional Planning*, Unwin Hyman, London.

Pearson, P.J.G., and P.J. Stevens, (1987). *Integrated Energy Forecasting and Policy in LDC's.*

Pindyck, R.S. and D.C. Rubinfield (1976). *Econometric Models and*

Economic Forecasts, , McGraw Hill, Kogakusha Ltd., Tokyo.

Poole, K.E., *Problems of Administration and Equity Under a Spending Tax*. American Economic Review, March 1943.

Pratibha, P.V. (1996). *Energy Ladder profile of All India Household Energy Demand in Rural and Urban Context. Ph.D. Thesis*. India: University of Hyderabad.

Pacific and Asian Journal of Energy, *Problems and Prospects*, Vol.I, Issue 1.

Qureshi, M.L. (1981), *Survey of Economic Resources and Prospects of South Asia*, Lotus Process Limited, Colombo.

Rahman, Sultan Nafeez, (1988). *Aggregate Energy Demand Projections in India: An Economic Approach*, Pacific and Asian Journal of Energy, Vol. II, Issue 1.

Rakshit, M. (1997). *Studies in the Macro Economics of Developing Countries*, Oxford University Press, Delhi.

Ranadive, K.R., *Income Distribution : the Unsolved Puzzle*, 1978.

Ranjitkar S.B.(1987). A note on Energy Policy of His Majesty's Government, the Nepalese Economic Journal Vol. 9, No. 4.

R. Bhardwaj, ..."Arth Vijnana", 1969, Vol. XI, No. I, p. 153.

Reddy,B. S., (1994). *A Multilogit Model for Fuel Shifts in the Domestic Sector*. Bombay: Indira Gandhi Institute of Development Research.

REDP (1990). *Rural Energy Statistics, Materials for a One-Week Training Programme*, Economic and Social Commission for Asia Pacific, Bangkok.

Rijal, Kamal (ed.), (1997). *Energy Use in Mountain Areas, Emerging Issues and Future Priorities*, Report of a Regional Meeting, ICIMOD.

Rijal, K., N. K. Bansal and P. D. Grover, (1990). *Rural Household Energy Demand Modelling: A Case Study of Nepal*. Energy Economics.

Rossi, N. (1988). *Government Spending, The Real Interest Rate and the Behaviour of Liquidity Constrained Consumers in Developing Countries*, IMF Staff papers, Vol. 35, Washington.

Roy P. (1973). *Appraisal and Control of Project Costs*, McGraw Hill, London.

Sen, A. (1987). *Poverty and Famines*, ELBS.

Shirley Mary, *The Experience with Privatization*, Finance and Development; A Quarterly Publication of IMF and World Bank,

September 1988, p. 34.

Shrestha, B.P., Jain, S.C., *Regional Development In Nepal: An Exercise in Reality*, Development Publishers, Delhi, 1978, p. 114.

Singer, H.W. and J.A. Ansari (1988). *Rich and Poor Countries*, Ukrin Hymam.

Socessan, J, (1988) Primary Sources of Energy on the Third World, Routledge, London.

Subbarao, K. *et al.* (1997) *Safety Net Programs and Poverty Reduction*, The World Bank, Washington D.C.

Swindell, K, J. M. Bada, M. J. Mortimore, (1989) *Inequality and Development*, Case Studies of the Third Word, Macmillan Publishers, London.

Thiel, H. (1970). *Economic Forecasts and Policy*, 2nd ed., Amsterdam.

Thirlwall, A.P. (1994) *Growth and Development*, Macmillan, Hongkong.

Timilsina, P. P., "*Planned Development in Nepal and Private Sector* (Nepali)", Mirmire, Nepal Rashtra Bank, Bankers Club 2045 B.S.

Tripathy, R.N., *Public Finance in Under-developed Countries*, 1985.

Turve, George Lewis (1976), Energy, Environment, Population and Food, John Willey, N.Y.

UNDP (1996, 1997). *Human Development Report*, Oxford University Press, New York.

UNDP/ WB, (1983). *Nepal: Issues and Options in Energy Sector, Report No. 4474-NEP*, UNDP/ WB.

UNDP/WEC (2000). *World Energy Assessment*, UNDP, NY.

United Nations, ECAFE, Economic Survey of Asia and Far East. 1953 to 1976.

..........Public Finance, Surveys of Iran, Iraq, India, Columbia and the Philipines, 1951.

UNO (1978) *A Guide to Practical Project Appraisal, Project Formulation and Evaluation*, Series No. 3, UNO, New York.

Veena, D.R., (1988). *Rural Energy*, Ashish Publishing House, Delhi.

Wallace,T.D. and A.Q. Hussain (1969). *The Use of Error Components Models in Combining Cross-Section with Time Series Data*, Econometrica Vol. 37.

WEC, (1993), *Energy for Tomorrow's World*, St. Martins Press, London.

WEC, (1993), *for Tomorrow's World*, St. Martins Press, London.

WEC-FAO (1999). *Rural Energy and Development Improving Energy Supplies for two million people*. Washington DC.

WECS (1984). *Energy Consumption in Transport Sector of Nepal*, Unpublished Report No. 4/1/2221184/1/1, Kathmandu, Nepal.

WECS (19?). *Electrical Energy Demand Forecasting Using Econometric Methods:* The Central Power System-1967/68 to 1976/77 with Projections to 1989/90.

WECS, (1992). *Sectoral Energy Demand for Nepal'* WECS, Kathmandu.

WECS, (1994 ,1996). *Energy Sector Synopsis Report*, WECS, Ministry of Water Resources, Kathmandu.

WECS, (1994). *Energy Sector Synopsis Report*, WECS, Ministry of Water Resources, Kathmandu.

———(1995). *Perspective Energy Plan, Supporting* Document no.2, 3,6,7, 9 and 10, WECS, Ministry of Water Resources, Kathmandu.

Weiss, D. (1976) *Economic Evaluation of Projects*, German Development Institute, Berlin.

William, J. G. (1965), *"Regional Inequality and Process of Development: A Description of the Patterns"*, Economic Development and Cultural Change, Vol. 13.

W.J. B..umal (1978). *Economic Theory and Operations Analysis*, Prentice Hall of India Pvt. Ltd., New Delhi, p. 538.

World Bank [1980]. *Energy in the Developing Countries*, World Bank, Washington D.C.

World Bank, (1983). *Energy Transition in Developing Countries*, NY.

World Bank (1983), Energy Transition in Developing Countries, Washington D.C.

World Bank (1986) *Poverty and Hunger*, Washington, D.C.

World Bank (1989). *Nepal: Policies for Improving Growth and Alleviating Poverty*, Washington, D.C.

World Bank (1990,1991, 1997, 2001). The World Development Report, Washington, D.C.

World Bank (1990). *Nepal Relieving Poverty in a Resource Scarce Economy*, Vol. I, Vol. II, WB/UNDO Study Report No. 8635.

Wionczed, N.S. and Ragai S. Nallakhed (1985). *Mexico's Energy Resources*, Westview press, Inc. USA.

.........(1993). Energy, *Efficiency and Conservation in the Third World*, Washington D.C.

World Energy Council (1993), *Energy for Tomorrow's World*, St. Martins Press, London.

... (1996). *Rural Energy and Development*, USA.

...(1993) *Energy, Efficiency and Conservation in the Developing World*, N.Y.

... (1996). *Rural Energy and Development, Improving Energy Supplies for Two Million People, The World Bank, USA.*

W.W. Leontief, The Structure of American Economy, 1919-39, Vora and Company Publishers Private Ltd., 1971, p. 207